Yolanda,

Thank you, than

For all your suppor... + know this
book will help you on your spiritual journey.
Much love,
—V.

ANCESTRAL MAJIK

*Creating Your Own Ancestral Deity
System*

V.V. Gunn

CreateSpace Independent Publishing

ANCESTRAL MAJIK

Copyright © 2017 by V.V. Gunn.

The information contained within this book is strictly for educational purposes only. If you wish to apply any of the methods/ideas contained within this book, you are fully responsible for your actions. V.V. Gunn is not accountable for your actions or any results of your actions from participating in any of the exercises/methods presented in this book.

For more information visit:
www.mysmajik.me

Cover created by Asia Campbell
ISBN: 978-1-9738-3947-7

First Edition: July 2017
CreateSpace Independent Publishing

C O N T E N T S

INTRODUCTION

From a young age, I've always been interested in magick and the occult. It wasn't until I entered college that I noticed that all my interest in mythology, horror and the supernatural were all occult topics.

My newfound interest in the occult was nurtured by great teachers such as Bobby Hemmitt and Brother Panic. The way in which they spoke about this subject matter with such confidence and ease – it captivated me and touched a primal part of me that longed to be released. Years later and after tons of research I created this comprehensive guide on how to access your primal power by diving head first into the underworld – the realm of the ancestors. Now, you may be thinking, "There are tons of books on ancestor worship, why would I need to read your book?" Great question; this book does not promote ancestor worship. Many books on the market today spew the same information over and over. You're told how to make a basic ancestor altar with a few trinkets; a glass of water, some food and a few favorite things.

Once your basic ancestor altar is completed, you petition them to help you solve the same human bullshit that really doesn't mean much in the grand scheme of things and that you can pretty much solve on your own if you'd just take the time out to do what you really need to do for yourself. This form of ancestor worship/veneration is great. I'm in no role to judge you for your spiritual practices but within these pages is an evolved perspective away from traditional ancestor worship/veneration. No longer will you be limited to dated ideologies. Revealed in the pages ahead are methods you can use to discover the ancient names of your beloved ancestors. Summon the power of your ancestors by learning how to craft personal rituals.

Open new dimensions of consciousness by communing with your ancestors with an elevated mindset. The depths of the realms you'll reach are limitless. Your ancestors don't have to be remembered for their mundane existence. Know that they are greater than any lifetime they've experienced! Now is an awesome time to dive deeper into the realm of the ancestors. The lid has been blown open on many forms of spirituality, you are no longer shamed for exploring different belief systems. Allow this book to expand your view of the afterlife, remove your old programming and allow the spirits of the underworld to guide you.

Countless ancestors populate the underworld and await your descent. Gain knowledge, wisdom and understanding of the universe and your role within it through communicating with those who know you best, your ancestors. Ancestral Majik is your guide to traverse these forgotten but familiar realms, allow me, Mys Majik to be your guide.

PRIMER

The Oxford Dictionary's definition of an ancestor states: "A person, typically one more remote than a grandparent, from whom one is descended." This definition correlates with the common and accepted understanding of what an ancestor is; a deceased person one shares a genetic link with. Anyone who you can place a direct genetic link from is your ancestor and is celebrated as such. But the purpose of this guide is not for you to become fixated with respecting and honoring just the deceased relatives of your bloodline but to gain interest and begin working with those you deem worthy of honoring no matter if they're related to you or not.

We must first understand that our ancestors are not dead. They continue to live on after physical death. Many ancient texts explain how this physical dimension, 3rd dimension, the life and world you've known is death. In the Qabalah, the world that we live in is known as Malkuth which means kingdom. It is defined as "the realm of matter/earth and relates to the physical world, the planets and solar system." A comprehensive explanation of Malkuth comes from Gareth Knight in his book, <u>A Practical Guide to Qabalistic</u>

Symbolism. He explains that Malkuth is birth and death. "By birth we come into the world and by death we go out into it. Birth and death however are two sides of the same coin, for when one dies physically, one is born into the higher world, and when one is born physically, from the point of view of higher worlds one is dead." Another way of looking at life as death, Knight writes;

"To the wider consciousness, the womb is a grave and the grave is a womb. The evolving soul, entering upon life, bids farewell to his friends who mourn him, and taking his courage in both hands and facing the great ordeal and submitting to suffering, enters upon life."

Death of physical life releases your essences, your soul from its prison – the physical body. Once you're no longer restricted by the flesh, you're released from limitation, no longer bound by physical laws, rules and insanity. Think about the world, how every living thing residing within this physical dimension must be subjected to the laws and rules of another. The one percent who rule the world use the power of their imagination to create the laws and status-quo that all are forced to live by. It is impossible in this dimension of matter to live in complete harmony and peace which is the deception that most people have been forced to believe.

No matter what your actions, good or bad, may in fact have a negative or positive outcome on someone else's life, no matter how big or small. Those water bottles you threw away in the trash will wind up polluting some body of water and may end up suffocating some random marine life who thought it was something to eat. Thus, causing disharmony within the aquatic kingdom and eco-system which creates a ripple effect that may throw everything out of whack. Just look at how pesticides have killed tons of bees which now threatens the planet's food supply since bees pollinate plants and most plants grow food. It is impossible to prevent bad things from happening in this dimension, these are just the rules of the game. Many people try to make it their life mission to prevent anything bad from happening. This is an idiot mission. Earth, physical dimension, 3rd dimension, whatever you want to call it will never be a perfect place because it is not our final-destination. It is not heaven, it is a place that should have never been created at all. Ancient myths ranging from Gnostic to Sumerian highlight topics about the soul, humanity and the creation of earth being an abomination.

Life is Death and Death is Life. Your perception keeps you trapped within the mode of thinking that continues to believe this illusionary world matters. What is perceived to be vital such as food, water, air, the human body – are merely an afterthought in the next world, the afterlife. You've been conditioned to believe that your physical life is the only thing that matters in the universe, that human existence is the highest attainment in the universe – wrong! It is a small step up the ladder of enlightenment, your journey being to know the fullest extent of your true self your higher self. The power of perception, creativity and imagination are the vital functions needed to realize your potential. These functions are also what is needed to access the realm of the ancestors. These are the same functions our ancestors use to navigate the underworld/afterlife.

Creativity, imagination and perception are crucial for navigating the spirit world. You and your ancestors have full access to this power now. Your imagination is so powerful it can even alter your perception allowing you to transcend the limits of this physical world only by the simple action of thought. Changing your thinking and how you perceive the world is critical to gnosis. The spiritual mysteries of the universe transcend logic although one can comprehend them through rational explanations. The experiences themselves are made clear through use of creativity and the imagination.

Your ancestors reside in the underworld which is nothing more than the deep dimensions of your subconscious mind. The underworld/afterlife is where the soul moves on to after death of the physical body. It is home to many planes of existence; Anything much higher than the physical universe. Your ancestors are like your personal army, they are always with you, they aid you on things you may not be aware of and are always ready to guide and express boundless love.

Your subconscious mind is where you can visit, communicate and interact with your ancestors. The subconscious mind is also the realm of dreams. The more creative you are the better and easier the communication will be between you and the dearly departed. The level of power and the way you perceive the power that your ancestors possess is based on their level of imagination and yours as well. A profound understanding of spiritual knowledge is beneficial. Since you're interested in this guide, it is a sure sign that you're highly proficient in spiritual topics whether you believe it or not. Your imagination is endless! With it, you have the power to mold your heaven and hell. You have the power to manifest you desires and shape your reality both in this world and the next.

Our ancestors can come to us in any form and help us in many ways dealing with our daily lives and even our spiritual evolution. Depending how ready you are to receive their call will determine how often they may try to communicate with you. But know this – they are always here with you, protecting and guiding you whether you are aware of it or not. We all have had experiences where our deceased loved ones have tried to contact us. Can you think of a few cases? While you reflect on those memories, below are listed a few personal experiences I've had with my very own ancestors.

Paw-Paw's Hat

When I was about four or five years old, I remember playing in my grandmother's bedroom while my aunt sat on the bed watching television. At some point during my play time I became interested in a small cardboard box near the door of my grandmother's room. An unexplainable force drew me towards it. The small cardboard box was open and inside was a brown fedora. As I examined the hat – it smelled like smoke. I remember picking the hat up and just looking at it and thinking it smelled funny. I then put the hat on my head. Trying to get my aunt's attention I noticed a man standing in the doorway of my grandmother's bedroom. I just stood still looking at the man in the doorway. He looked down at me with a smile and said, "Oh, you found my hat." I don't remember saying anything back. He then said, "I'm your Paw-Paw, everything is okay." After that the memory gets a little hazy. All I remember after that is turning away from the door and looking at my aunt who didn't notice anything since she was still watching television. I walked up to her and she looked at me and said, "This is paw-paw's hat." When I looked back to the door the man wasn't there anymore. Thinking back, I don't remember feeling fear. The man – my paw-paw gave off a warm and loving feeling. The last thing I remember is telling my aunt, "I know it's his hat, he told me it was." Once I told her that she just looked at me a bit shocked and then went downstairs I think to tell my grandmother.

The cool thing about this story is that I never met my paw-paw. He died two years before I was born. For me at such a young age to tell my aunt that I knew whose hat it was – is still a profound experience for me and was my first introduction with spirits and ancestors.

Below is another story about the time when my Uncle Doug's spirit came to visit. I was a lot older by this time, just finished my third year in college. On top of school work, I'd been studying new age topics such as meditation, chakras and gnosticism. This was a time when I was becoming more receptive and open to my innate spiritual abilities.

Midnight Cravings

I had just finished writing a screenplay for one of my classes. To celebrate I decided to cook myself a midnight victory dinner. Looking through the fridge I couldn't find anything that I wanted to eat. The fridge was well-stocked because my mom went grocery shopping a few days before. I had a craving for something but couldn't really pinpoint what type of food I was craving. I'm sure we all have those mystery cravings and at this moment I was experiencing a heavy one. I opened the refrigerator again, scanning the selves. A white coffee mug caught my eye. Upon looking and smelling the contents it turned out to be bacon grease. Suddenly a loaf of wheat bread caught my eye on the shelf below and I could feel my hunger getting stronger. This is what I'd been craving. I fired up a small skillet, loaded a few scoops of the bacon grease and toasted a few pieces of bread in the grease. Just as my "meal" was finishing my mom walks into the kitchen asking me what was cooking. As I placed the bread onto my plate and before I could answer she says, "I know you're not about to eat that!" I looked at her and she had a bit of a surprised expression on her face. I told her, "I don't know why but I just feel like eating this." My mother begins to laugh before saying, "You know, my brother...your Uncle Doug used to eat his bread like this all the time."

Just like the physical manifestation of my grandfather. Our ancestors can make their presence known in a variety of ways based on the individual who they are trying to contact and the power of their imagination. The last story I will share happened after I graduated college and was completely invested in my occult studies and been experiencing success in my rituals.

Family Reunion

I recently finished reading Robert Moss' book, <u>The Dreamer's Book of the Dead</u>. His words gave me the information and motivation to try and contact my dearly departed love ones. I quickly decided that I wanted to talk to my older brother Zandor. I followed the instructions stated in the section of Moss' book titled 'Journey to the Departed.' Moss instructed that before going to sleep, repeat to yourself that you will visit your dearly departed in the dream world. For a couple of nights, before going to sleep I repeated over and over that, "I want to talk to my brother Zandor." The first couple of nights of doing this ritual I didn't remember anything about my dreams. At this point in my life, I didn't remember much of any of my dreams. So, not remembering if I'd spoken to my brother or not wasn't such a big deal; Still motivated and determined to make contact I repeated this exercise for three more nights before drifting off to dreamland. On the morning of the fourth day, I finally remembered my dream. I was back in my grandmother's old house, the one where I met my paw-paw for the first time. This time I was my current age and not a child. There was a cookout going on and my entire family was around. I walked through the house looking at everyone and everything. My mom and all my aunts were in the kitchen cooking, my dad and uncles were in the yard tending to the grill. My sisters were chilling in the living room talking. My nieces and nephews were running around the house playing. More family played and talked in the front yard. After looking around I didn't find my brother Zan. I asked around and everyone said they hadn't seen him. At this point I felt a little sad because the person I'd been working so hard to see again wasn't even here! Just as I ventured into the living room to sit down my cellphone started to ring (I had no idea I had my cellphone) and the caller I.D. read, Zan. I picked up the phone and heard his voice as clear as ever. I was overjoyed! Finally, I had contact and was seeing the fruits of my labor. I asked him where he was and was he coming to the party. He told me he couldn't make it because he was studying. I asked him what is he studying and he told me, "The Stars."

Early in my occult studies I found that stars = souls. In ancient cultures, it was believed that the stars are linked to the soul. Famous occultist Aleister Crowley states in his book, The Book of the Law, *"Every man and every woman is a star."* Once I awoke from my dream I knew exactly what Zandor was talking about. He was studying his soul, learning various things about himself and his power. After meeting my brother in the dream world. The presence of my ancestors became very real for me. That dream experience allowed me to become aware of constant blessing my ancestors give regularly. Offering daily protection and abundance in the form of money and knowledge.

I've had numerous experiences that I would love to go into more detail about but I'm sure you get my point. Your ancestors are here, they've always been here. They've been helping you and will continue to do so. Once you answer their call and become aware of their presence and begin to strengthen your relationship then that's when you begin to awaken your true power.

ANCESTOR WORSHIP AROUND THE WORLD

For thousands of years, people all over the world celebrate their ancestors. In modern times, Halloween is an unofficial day of celebration of the ancestors and spirits. This is a time when the veil between the spirit world and physical world is weakest thus allowing spirits easy access to communicate with the living. October 31st isn't the only day where the souls of the dead are most active and Halloween isn't the only day to celebrate the ancestors. Listed below are a few cultures and customs where spirits of the dead have been celebrated for centuries.

<u>Ancient Egypt</u>

Death had an everlasting presence in the daily life of the Ancient Egyptian. These Ancient Ancestors believed and documented their belief in the afterlife in every aspect of their lives. It was common belief that the soul lived on after the death of the physical body. Death was so important to them that they took great precaution when handling the deceased and praising their Ancestors. The rituals used to honor the dead differed depending on the class and wealth of the family of the deceased. Royal and wealthy Egyptians dedicated extravagant offerings in the form of food and gifts which were placed in temples to the deceased. Prayers and hymns were recited to ease the departed into their new life in the next realm. For those who weren't wealthy or of royal blood the act of offering food and prayers remained the same but to a lesser degree. A small statue was created and placed within or near the home and offerings were placed near the statue. As a reward the recently deceased or ancestors would help with any difficulties plaguing the family. A popular festival known as, The Wag Festival, took place around (what would be known as) August 17th – 19th. In honor of the Lord of the Underworld Osiris; where plenty of food and alcohol was given to all those who participated in honoring Osiris and the ancestors.

West Africa

In the Ifa religion, the concept of death resembles that of the Ancient Egyptians. That death is a process, that one moves from this world into another. Ancestors are buried near the home instead of a cemetery. What the ancestors enjoyed in life will be made as an offering. Meals are prepared and dedicated to them. Cleaning the grave, lighting candles and talking to them near the grave are ways used to honor the ancestors. Altars are created with a white table cloth, a glass of water (up to nine glasses), pictures (optional), alcohol (usually rum) and prayer. The ancestors are petitioned to help with relationships, health, finances and anything else that needs assistance in the life of their descendants.

China

Ancestor worship has been practiced since the days of the Xia Dynasty 2070 - 1060 B.C. It was common belief that prosperity is given to those who honor their ancestors and but if one committed ill deeds and behavior they would be looked down upon by the ancestors and no blessings will be received. In the ancient cultures of China (and even still today) it was believed that the ancestors had direct contact with various gods and goddesses. The ancestors could petition for favors from the gods and goddesses to benefit their descendants. To honor and keep in good favor with the ancestors, maintaining their graves, offering food, incense, beverages and various other trinkets would keep the individual and family in good standing with their ancestors. In ancient and modern times, a family altar is placed within a home in the form of small temple or shrine. The sizes of the altars vary from a table or shelf in the corner of a room or even an entire room. Spirit money also referred as Joss Paper or Hell Notes, is burned to aid in the transformation of the dead in the afterlife. Burning

Joss Paper also appeases spiritual debts and gives ancestors a way to afford nice items that will make them comfortable in the afterlife. It is still common belief that if the dead/ancestors are not honored then they transform into hungry ghosts and haunt the living. Festivals take place each year to make sure that the dead/ancestors are remembered and provided for.

The Ghost Festival: spirits from other realms and ancestors are said to wander around during this time. Elder ancestors are worshipped during this time. They are given spirit money, incense, and food. Hungry ghost wander around for food; food and performances such as plays are given to entertain them.

The Chinese New Year: offerings in the form of the ancestors' favorite food are placed on an altar inside the home along with incense. Respect is given to the deceased ancestors as well as the living elders. The same reverence is given to the many gods and goddesses of the Chinese pantheon.

Clear and Bright Festival: the graves/tombs of the ancestors are swept and food, tea, prayer and the burning of joss paper are offered. On this day, all ancestors of various ages and generations are respected and remembered.

The United States

In the African American spiritual system known as Hoodoo, the act of ancestor worship has blended many traditions from Native Americans to West African. Ancestors related by blood or not can be honored. Many root-workers in traditions such as Hoodoo believe that ancestors live on in another realm and assist us in our times of need. An altar is created as a vessel to offer food and gifts which varies depending on the individual. Creating an altar allows one to build a spiritual connection with the deceased and develop spiritual allies. A traditional Hoodoo ancestor altar includes a table with or without a table cloth (usually a white table cloth), a glass of water, white candles, flowers and pictures of your ancestors. Rum, whiskey or other alcohol may be placed on the altar, usually what the ancestor(s) enjoyed while living is placed in this sacred space. Cigarettes, cigars, coffee, and sweets are also placed on the altar. Items that belonged to the dearly departed can be placed on the altar as well. A prayer and petition is recited to the ancestors to welcome them.

Mexico

Ancestor worship in Mexico dates back even before the days of the Mayan Empire. Much information covering the ancient Mayan ancestor worship traditions hasn't been recorded although some information exists. The ancient Mayans believed that the spirits of the ancestors lived on after death. Ancestors were to be admired and respected and a very noble way of showing love to an ancestor was through the ritual of bloodletting. Royals were often placed into pyramids consisting of nine platforms simulating the nine planes of the afterlife/consciousness. It isn't said if the Mayans offered food, beverages or anything else to their ancestors. Bundles of precious objects belonging to the ancestors have been found by archaeologists in recent years.

The Day of the Dead begins October 31st and ends November 2nd[t]. On the starting day of the festival, prayers are recited for the souls of children while the second day is reserved for the souls of adults. The Day of the Dead has been practiced for thousands of years by the indigenous people of Mesoamerica. The festivities include visits to cemeteries where flowers are laid on the graves of the departed. Families clean and decorate the graves of loved ones with their favorite items and food. Skulls and skeletons are decorated lavishly and displayed around the community, neighborhoods and city. Altars are created for the ancestors; usually a table draped with a cloth. Various items are placed on the altar such as candles, incense, marigold flowers, fresh fruit, pictures of the honored dead, and food including a dish known as "Bread of the Dead."

There are many more cultures and customs that celebrate ancestors to be explored. Ancestor worship is common around the world for millennia. I hope this information motivates you to learn more about other customs and gives you plenty of ideas to add to your own rituals.

It has been said throughout the black conscious community that all indigenous people (black people) are gods and goddesses. History (ancient and modern) as well as genetics support this belief. I agree with both of my teachers Bobby Hemmitt and Brother Panic, when they state that we as the original people of this planet and creators of the known and unknown universe are above god. To call yourself a god is but a splash in the pond of your true potential and power. Both teachers refer to us as chaos beings which helps to suggest not only our primal power as black people but also the primal power our ancestors which we now have total access to because they are no longer bound to a human body and the laws of this physical dimension.

In the next section I will highlight traits that will help to boost your confidence in your primal power and recognize yourself as a chaos being.

YOU ARE GOD

"Breath allows the Ancestors to rise within us and for us to descend within them." – Bobby Hemmitt

"Your god is within you, so make use of it." – Phillip Cooper

The universal idea of god is; the creator and lord of creation and the universe. God is a supernatural being or force that is worshipped by many for his powers over the elements, nature, events and humanity. You have the same abilities – you can manipulate events so that the outcome is in your favor, change people's thoughts and feelings and manifest prosperity or whatever your heart desires. Using deities and spirits helps you to manifest your will. These gods and goddesses that have been worshipped for years and by many cultures are nothing but various attributes of your inner power.

Deities such as Lakshmi, Isis, Lilith and many more are energies created by you to catalog and illustrate your primal power. You are nothing more than the same energy frozen in matter (a human body). Your ancestors are attached to the very same energy. The only difference is that your ancestors once occupied a human body possibly for many lifetimes. Many believe these popular deities to reside in another realm (Heaven) traveling to those who call and honor them. What prevents your ancestors from illustrating the same feats? They too reside in another realm often depicted as Heaven; when they were "alive" in a physical body they had the same power to manipulate their reality to their standards. Since "death" is only the transition between one plane of existence to the next, wouldn't they possess the same power to manipulate events but now on an even greater scale since they are no longer bound to the laws of humanity and this physical dimension?

You and your ancestors are more than god, chaos beings are more fitting to describe your primal power. The afterlife/underworld is where your ancestors reside. To descend into the underworld is to tap into your subconscious mind. This is your powerhouse that completes the tasks of your will. You hold your own destiny and life in your own hands. Ancestors, spirits, deities, etc. can be found in your imagination, the realm of your subconscious mind.

There are tons of spiritual and religious texts to decode that explain how and why you are god and/or how to become one. Instead of including many excerpts from various sources and explaining many terms. The five basic elements: fire, earth, air, water and ether (spirit) are found within the bodies of all melanated people. These elements are comprised in the human body as:

Earth – Bones, teeth, organs, hair and nails.

Fire – Digestive enzymes in our body used to digest food and create energy/fuel.

Water – Up to 70% of the human body is water. Urine, mucus and blood are all comprised of water.

Air – Oxygen and metabolism.

Ether – Spirit; what animates your body and all living things.

These elements help the physical body to function. These elements correspond with spiritual elements. The five elements that make an individual into a god/chaos being are:

Fire - Kundalini

The spiritual energy, kundalini is within everything in the universe. It is a cosmic energy vital for spiritual enlightenment. Although having raised and balanced kundalini energy does not equal automatic spiritual enlightenment, it is an essential step to attaining spiritual understanding of the universe and your place within it. The first steps to activating this energy starts in the base chakra located at the seat of the spine; from there the kundalini energy rises from the base chakra (located at the 4th lumbar vertebrae) to each chakra until finally resting at the top of the skull, where the crown chakra is located. Kundalini goes by other names such as Chi, Ki and Shakti. The spiritual benefits of Kundalini energy are; enhanced psychic abilities, creativity, sexual energy, powerful aura, compassion/empathy, spiritual connection and purification. It helps to awakening your pineal gland. Besides the spiritual benefits of kundalini energy, it also helps the physical body ward off illness, slows aging and helps to keep one mentally and emotionally balanced. Shakti energy is described as your inner Goddess and the feminine force that rules the universe. In Barbara G. Walker's book, Women's Myths and Secrets, kundalini energy is described as:

"Tantric image of the female serpent coiled in the lowest chakra of the human body, in the pelvis. An aim of Tantric yoga was to "realize Kundalini" by certain exercises and meditations, such as yoni-mudra: contractions of the perineal muscles, training men to suppress ejaculation. If Kundalini could be induced to uncoil and mount through the spinal chakras to the brain, the adept would experience bliss of her emergence as the "thousand-petaled lotus" from the top of the head, which mount union of the self with the infinite. Tibetan lamas still consider the most secret, sacred mantra the one that wakens the sleeping Kundalini and causes her to rise."

Air – Soul

Can you describe air? One can explain its properties, what it's made of - but can you fully describe it? Now on the flipside, try to describe the soul. What is the soul? One can explain different functions of the soul but without explaining those functions, no words can explain what the soul truly is. The mere idea of the soul is what it represents.

The human body cannot survive on this physical plane without air. Without a soul, one cannot exist beyond the physical plane and traverse the vast spiritual realms. No soul = nonexistence. The soul is the battery that allows all to operate. It is our inspiration to create new things, our imagination that makes any and everything worthwhile. Without inspiration, creativity and imagination to create new ideas and conceive new concepts, one would live a soulless life.

Our thoughts are birthed from an unlimited source (the subconscious mind), the soul is the battery that powers this function. In Symbols and Sacred Objects by Barbara G. Walker it's states that:

"Jesus's assertion that "the Kingdom of God is within you" (Luke 17:21) filtered down from Ionian philosophers of the 6th and 5th centuries B.C. They identified the air-soul as God, and proposed that the divine spark within man was precisely the air he breathed, the "finest" element, forming the personal soul and the Oversoul at the same time. The philosophers reasoned that if God = air = soul, then the air within a breathing person was an inner God judging the actions—an interior conscience. Christians largely accepted the air-soul theory, drawing out of it their ideas of invisible ghosts that could be felt but not seen, like air; and the notion that the soul can depart the body through the nose or mouth."

The soul is also believed to be comprised of sulfur, a union of both air and fire. Described as hot, moveable and penetrating just like air or a flame. Chemical Sulfur produces a fierce bright flame when ignited. The soul is often depicted as a bright ball of light.

Water - Blood

Menstrual blood (also known as Soma & Ambrosia) has been regarded as the most powerful substance in the world by mystics in ancient cultures. Known as the blood of immortality, modern science has discovered that women's menses carry stem cells; regenerating cells thus innovating modern science. In many myths, it is said that the blood of gods was used to create humans. The Babylonian myth of Tiamat and Kingu explains how after a great battle with Marduk, the blood of Kingu was mixed with earth and used as clay to create humans while Tiamat's body created the sky and earth. In ancient Sumerian texts, it is stated that menstrual blood is the "gold of the gods." Sacrificing blood was often used as a gift to appease the gods and connect with them. Barbara G. Walker again with dynamite information about the wonders and power of menstrual blood states in her book, Man Made God: A Collection of Essays, she goes on to say that:

> "The Maori stated that all humans are made of menstrual blood. Africans "knew" that menstrual blood retained in the womb was what made a baby. Indians of South America declared that all humanity was created in the beginning by the Great Mother's 'moon blood.' The Chinese called it the 'red yin juice' that gives life to all things, from time immemorial controlled by the Moon Goddess Chang-O."

Walker continues, "The bible specifically states that the life of all flesh is in its blood (Lev 17:11) and calls menstrual blood the "flower" of the womb (Lev 15:24), corresponding to the child it produces which is the 'fruit' of the womb (Psalm 127:3). The bible calls menstrual blood 'unclean' as a translation of the Latin **sacer** (sacred, holy), which actually meant 'taboo' – a substance both sacred and dreadful, with the power to bring down the very gods themselves."

Popular gods are associated with the power of menstrual blood. Ogun the god of iron mourns menstruation since it signals the failure of a child being born. Also within Ogun's mysteries is a red powder known as Irosun which is used to consecrate an Ogun pot. Irosun is red camwood powder which is used as a substitute of menstrual blood to mimic its primal reproductive power. Red cloths and red rust from iron spikes are also items used for Ogun's pot. Banded iron formations (which are red in color) are millions of years old and formed in sea water; were found as the source of the first cell life forms on Earth – thus metaphorically illustrating menstrual blood and its power.

Earth - Melanin

Melanin is a wonderful enigma. It's a treasure, a natural mineral that supports your body and all its functions. The Earth is a vessel that gives us access to many resources and objects that are vital to our physical existence such as fire, water, food, plants, insects, animals and tons more. The physical nature of melanin is what gives you and all humans the pigment in the skin, eyes and hair. It also assists with your sight, hearing and central nervous system. Besides being your glorious armor providing protection from harmful substances, melanin has many divine properties. According to Dr. Richard King (who is a scholar on melanin), he states in his book, Melanin: A Key to Freedom:

"Melanin is the chemical of life – of the soul. A doorway through which the energy waves of the holy soul, spirit and mind pass to take form. It produces inner vision, true spiritual consciousness, creative genius (godlike qualities) and the ability to have conversations with the immortals."

There is so much information available on the wonders of melanin. Entire books have been written on this subject and it would take an entire book to explain all of melanin's wonders. But, in a nutshell melanin is one the primary physical manifestations of your primal powers.

Ether/Spirit = Pineal Gland

"The seat of the soul is the pineal gland." -Descartes

The pineal gland produces Melatonin which is nothing more than melanin released throughout the entire body. The pineal gland is associated with diverse supernatural abilities. Also, referred to as the third eye or Ajna Chakra. The meaning of the word Anja is unlimited power. Many texts state that once the pineal gland is completly activated one enters a state of non-duality. A calm state of inner stillness with oneself and the universe. No longer does one feel separated or segregated. It is a place possible to manifest your desires and produce visions of the past, present and future. The pineal gland is also known as the seat of the soul.

The pineal gland can be associated with a sphere on the Qlippoth known as Daath (the abyss). Kenneth Grant is an author who states that, "Daath is the outer gateway to the Mauve Zone." In Peter Levenda's book, The Dark Lord, he states:

"According to Grant, the Mauve Zone is the source of all human creativity, imagination, fascination and obsession. It is represented in the microcosm by a zone that exists between the dream state and the deeper, dreamless state, and is the source of artistic impulse and contact with divine and demonic forces."

The Mauve Zone is the subconscious mind and the pineal gland (Daath) is the gateway to access its primal powers. Daath, the Mauve Zone is the ancestral realm. Daath is the gateway into the abyss.

Occultist and eschatologist, Brother Panic states in his book, The Origins of Occult Civilization Volume One: Hollywood;

"The pineal gland is considered your gateway to other realities. The labyrinth in occult understanding is considered the brain itself. You must find this gateway of light in the maze you call your brain; the pineal gland is the light at the end of your tunnel, it is Lucifer, the light bringer."

Ultimately, the five elements explained above can be used interchangeably. One term can describe many things and many can explain one thing. Think of these elements as symbols and as symbols they are used to express the primal power of both you and your ancestors. These five components; Kundalini, Soul, Blood, Melanin and Pineal are the basic equipment of a chaos being.

There are many magickal systems that explain how the human body is vehicle of god. Terms like "The Great Work" is one way to explain the journey of consciousness one must venture to realize the soul's role in the universe and re-connect to god-consciousness. Systems like the Qabalah illustrates how the Tree of Life can be compared to the human body with each sephiroth corresponding with a chakra and the left, middle and right side of the tree equates to the left, spine and right side of the human body. The sephiroth can also be looked at as levels of consciousness; various states/modes of thinking/feeling that one goes through on their spiritual journey. Opposite of the Qabalah is the "darker" side known as the Qlippoth/Tree of Knowledge/Death. Writer and occultist Kenneth Grant summarizes the Qlippoth perfectly with this statement from his book, <u>Nightside of Eden</u>:

"The Underworld domain of the backside of the Tree of Life (Qlippoth) is populated with the dead ancestors, gods and goddesses of the underworld, and the various demonic and sub-elemental spirits and powers."

Phillip Cooper in his book, <u>The Magickian</u>, advice for creating your own god is:

"In the search for the real god you must first reject all the others. Start with nothing and using constructive thought, build up your idea of what God ought to be for you. Any negative or restricted ideas must be avoided. Creativity is the keyword. Your god must be creative not destructive. Using your imagination, you build up a picture of God. You identify with the image, and by belief in this image, you eventually control maximum power. Whatever you believe in invariably comes true, so start to believe in something real. Start by removing everything, then after careful deliberation, start to reassemble or replace slowly and gradually. Keep the goal in mind: the real God is within you. Contacting your own true god is vitally important in the creative scheme that Magick seeks to reveal to you."

In the next section of this book, you will venture into the part where it will prepare you to reconnect with your ancestors on a primal and powerful level. Most of the ancestors have tapped into their primal power and are waiting for you to do the same. Your physical and spiritual journey has you appointed as the hero. As the hero, you're on a mythical adventure with weapons, armor, healing and magical items (the five elements listed above) all at your disposal. All these tools are essential in your journey. You give meaning to the world around you. Only those with the power of god could complete such a task.

BUILDING YOUR ANCESTRAL DEITY SYSTEM

Now it's time to get down to the nitty gritty and begin to craft your own ancestral deity system. We've covered many topics that should put to rest your questions about how you and your ancestors are powerful primal entities. From briefly explaining the concept of death and the afterlife to giving personal examples on how ancestors on the other side can make themselves known to you – to explaining your own magical tools that you hold within yourself; breathing life into the how and why you and your ancestors are gods in your own right with your own universes.

The purpose behind creating your own ancestral deity system is to empower your ancestors and yourself. Everything included in this section of this guide has been tested and yields great results to those who try them out. Feel free to adjust anything that is mentioned in the steps below to your own needs and ideas. Also, be aware that the results, revelations and answers you'll receive will vary; don't expect the same outcomes given in this guide. Be open to your own answers and experiences. Build your ancestral deity system with no expectations. The yearning and excitement of wanting to reconnect, find out more about the afterlife and the power your ancestors hold - the power that you also hold will guide you. Remember, your ancestors are powerful and so are you!

STEP 0: COMING TO TERMS

Before you begin your journey into the realm of the ancestors. You must first deal with any residual thoughts and feelings you have about death and the deceased that you wish to connect with. The foundation you must set is coming to terms with their passing. The ancestors you may be trying to contact may have been dead for years but as you begin to make contact with the other-side; old emotions, feelings of sadness and/or pain will begin to arise – and that's okay! It is perfectly normal to experience these emotions and you should. Grieve as much as you can no matter how long it has been since your dearly departed has passed. Do whatever it takes to allow your emotions to run their course. One of the things I recommend is that you write a letter, two letters. One to yourself, explaining your feeling during your grieving period. Just write any and everything that comes to mind. Such as:

- What happened to the person that is causing you to feel this way.
- Any regrets or fond memories of the person or people you are mourning.

Write whatever comes to mind. The second letter will be addressed to your dearly departed. In this letter, write whatever you wish to write about that deals with the ancestor(s) you're trying to connect with. If you are angry with them – tell them. If you're happy about them not being here in this physical dimension anymore, it is perfectly fine to express it. Make sure to explain yourself in detail. Once you've completed both letters, the next step is take each letter and read it aloud every day until you come to terms with the passing of your beloved ancestors and residual feelings surrounding their death. Doing this will allow you to release all that pent-up energy you have surrounding your ancestors. This will help ease your overall thoughts about death. You will repeat this process every day until you are ready to move on, remember just take your time. Once you are ready to move on, now is the time to complete your grieving ritual. Take both the letters you wrote, get a candle of any color, I prefer pink since it is the color of love. Grab a bowl, plate or tray, light the candle and begin reading each letter for one last time. Put on appropriate music, whatever represents the emotions you are experiencing. When you are finished reading both letters, place them in the flames of the candle and watch them burn to ash (place them in your bowl or tray to catch the ashes). You have now released those emotions you've had locked up inside of you into the universe. Now you are ready to do start your ancestral deity system!

Doing this ritual helps you to release any emotions you've been dealing with since the passing of your beloved ancestor. It also helps you come to terms with the act of death itself. Once you make the leap into communicating with your ancestors you know for a fact that death is not the end but indeed the beginning of something greater!

Letting go is the critical beginning step into developing your own ancestral deity system. As stated before, your idea of the afterlife and what goes on in that realm is all based around your thoughts, feelings and imagination. Deeply grieving and never coming to terms with the death of a loved one will cause that person great discomfort in the hereafter, due to the energy you continue to project towards them. If you are unhappy then they are unhappy. If you are hurting then they are hurting. Low emotions such as anger, grief and rage can keep the souls of the deceased trapped between dimensions. The grief, sorrow and anger you continue to project can prevent an ancestor from truly moving on. There are even ancestors who refuse to move on even after low emotions and thoughts have been eliminated. They continue to hold on due to their own feelings of anger, fear and sorrow. Thus, is why your imagination and intention are important. Staying genuine and true to yourself are the keys to liberating yourself; keeping unwanted energies at bay. Acknowledging your thoughts and feelings; changing them so that they always benefit you for the better is essential. Why continue to stay angry or sad at the past – it only creates disharmony and negativity which fuels all things around you including people, emotions, thoughts and perception. Your ancestors will greatly benefit from your piece of mind if they too are operating from higher emotions and thoughts. Typically, the ancestors that are eager to work with you are operating from a similar emotional and mental disposition.

Your journey into the realm of the ancestors will be an exciting one. It will not be free of uncomfortable emotions and experiences, but once you make the effort and take the steps to settle and come to terms with your emotions, everything will follow your lead. On this journey, old emotions and memories will continue to arise but do not run away, welcome them, acknowledge them and let them go. You will not only be one step closer to your true primal self but your ancestor(s) will too.

Cleansing and balancing your chakras will place you on a steady path of coming to terms with your ancestors, death and emotional wounds. Each chakra corresponds with an emotional/mental issue.

Root Chakra: Survival, acceptance, stability, self-preservation, fear, safety and perception.

Unbalanced/Blocked: Tiredness, obesity, hoarding, materialism, greed, can't deal with change, financial trouble and fear of safety.

Balanced: Vitality, feeling safe, trust, well grounded, stable and good health.

Sacral Chakra: Sexuality, emotions, finances and creativity.

Unbalanced/Blocked: addicted to sex, manipulative, addiction of any kind, emotional dependency, fear of sex, lack of passion, poor social skills and unwillingness to change.

Balanced: Abundance, pleasure, happiness, inner strength, creativity, balanced mood and emotions, healthy libido and pleasurable sex.

Solar Plexus Chakra: Personal power, self-esteem and connection with inner self.

Unbalanced/Blocked: Poor self-esteem/confidence, aggression, power hungry, control freak, victimization, lack of accountability, blaming others, overly competitive.

Balanced: Self-acceptance, cheerful, non-judgmental, empowered, doesn't worry, personal growth, productive and respect for others.

Heart Chakra: Forgiveness, unconditional love, peace, low or no stress, acceptance of past, connection with self and others.

Unbalanced/Blocked: Lack of self-respect and love, guilty, aloof, paranoid, clingy/needy, selfish, self-pity, intolerant of others, need constant reassurance and perfectionist.

Balanced: Full of joy, at peace, trust in yourself and others, nurturing of self and others, accepting of self and others, compassionate to self and others, loves yourself completely, no fear of rejection, forgiving, showing and feeling unconditional love, mind/body/spirit are balanced.

Throat Chakra: Change, honesty/truthfulness, inspiration/creativity, communication/self-expression, transformation and healing.

Unbalanced/Blocked: difficult to express self, lump in throat, choking back words/sobs, constant lying, passive aggressive behavior, ignorance, arrogance, constant chatter, difficult listening to others, fear of public speaking, argumentative, throat problems (sore throat, neck problems, constant mucus), temper tantrums and manipulative.

Balanced: Great communication in all forms, good at hearing and listening, appropriately speaks up, no second guessing, freely expresses self, speaks with confidence and passion and open to change.

Third Eye Chakra: Intuition, psychic abilities, higher consciousness, wisdom and pineal gland activity.

Unbalanced/Blocked: Illogical, lack of insight, lack of imagination/visualizing, stuck in your own head, too logical, fear of success and being wrong, fear of self and truth, can't manifest desires, pessimistic, materialism and constant worrying.

Balanced: Intuitive, open-minded, psychic, trusting your own intuition, optimistic, perceptive, calm mind, sleeps well, spiritual, able to see past illusion and into truth, aware and good dream recall.

Crown Chakra: Bliss, oneness, inspired, spiritual connection, divine understanding/awareness, high spiritual energy, balanced well-being and selflessness.

Unbalanced/Blocked: Constant worry, stress, depression, frustration, indecisive, indifferent, out of touch with reality, fear of death, lack of faith, lack of perceptiveness/high consciousness, schizophrenia, multiple personality disorder, lack of inspiration, feeling disconnected from spiritual source, headaches/migraines and hot/cold personality.

Balanced: Psychic, intuitive, freedom, awareness, not attached to physical dimension, sense of oneness, divine connection, access to subconscious/unconscious mind, no fear of death, love for life, spiritual guidance, good decision making, knowing "you live in this world but are not of it;" wise and at peace.

A great book to read about how one's psychological development is governed by each chakra is a book by John Nelson titled, <u>Healing the Split: Integrating Spirit into Our Understanding of the Mentally Ill</u>. Corresponding with the chakra system as psychic phenomenon known as mental/emotional images (MEI). In the book, <u>You Are Psychic</u>, author and psychic Debra Katz explains MEI's as;

> "Mental/Emotional Images are concentrated pockets of emotional energy and corresponding thoughts/ideas/beliefs that have accumulated in a certain location of our body. These pockets of energy are formed over time and are records of our experiences with corresponding feelings and thoughts about the experiences. They are frames of reference that motivate and control human perception; they dictate the manner in which people interpret and react to every aspect of life. Some MEI pictures are born from an initial emotionally charged or traumatic experience. Oftentimes they were created centuries ago during a person's former incarnation (past life). This experience forms a core of energy that acts like a magnet for similar experiences and energies. Over time this collection of experiences can have a snowball effect. They can become extremely emotionally charged and have quite a strong influence on one's perceptions, attitude and lifestyle."

It is important to remove these emotional pockets that hinder you in your life. Due to traumatic experiences whether they are big or small, if not properly exercised and removed, they can cause grief and mishaps in our lives. No matter how many times you ignore the insult you received as a child from someone, that insult may still play over and over in your head, awakening an emotion (usually negative) with that experience. Many people hold onto issues revolving around their parents that has caused them to adapt behavior based upon this trauma. Many men and women hate other men and women due to ill feelings related to ones' parents or adults that corresponds with the sex their anger is directed towards. MEIs create blocks in chi/kundalini energy in parts of our bodies and aura. These blocks create weakness in our energy field allowing other energies to take advantage of this vulnerable spot, plugging into our energy and allowing the same cycles of trauma to repeat themselves in our life, thoughts and emotions. Cleansing and balancing your chakras is essential! The vulnerable pockets within our energy fields attract people who will take advantage of these weak spots and the people that our weak spots attract are usually people who have the same vulnerable spots in their energy. The next time you ask yourself why you seem to attract the same type of people in your life, you must begin to look at your own trauma and flaws in your thinking and energy field/aura.

Another aspect of Mental/Emotional Images that takes on a grander scale is the energy of a generation. The energy of a generation has the power to dictate the human behavior and perceptions of a person. The social, emotional, mental and spiritual behavior of a generation is supplied by the planets and zodiac. The zodiac and planets are just expressions of energy that has the power to control human emotions and behavior. Many things that happen within a generation affects the people within that generation that fuels their MEIs. The planet, Pluto corresponds with Scorpio in the zodiac. Pluto is the god of the underworld (the subconscious). In Astrology, it is said that Pluto's powers are transforming, governing renewal and rebirth. Pluto is said to rule all that is "below the surface." Pluto is the planet of power; on AlwaysAstrology.com, it states that:

"Pluto is all about secret and undercover information. When it all comes to light, your world is changed. It is often considered to rule the masses more than the individual. Pluto may bring an end to things that need to be let go of. Pluto deals with social and personal power and powerlessness. Old hurts can build up, leaving us feeling powerless and victimized. This is Pluto at work. It attempts to compensate and pushes us to re-evaluate painful events and feelings. Once we do, we can attain a higher level of enlightenment and happiness. The message of your Pluto sign is Self-Empowerment. Look inward and examine what is there. Pluto will continue to push your buttons until you examine yourself and deal with what you find. It wants you to evolve and become more than what you are."

Everyone has an individual Pluto sign in their own astrology chart that helps to give answers to many issues in ones' life. But, let's examine the Pluto signs of generations that work to bring to light many psychological issues that plague generations but often get overshadowed by many social issues that work to impact the psyche of a generation. Thus, creating greater traumas that fuel the MEI's of a generation causing cycles of trauma to continue and never getting exorcised and resolved.

Let's look at a few generations to get a perspective on the thoughts, ideas and beliefs of a generation that still impacts their psychological behavior.

Pluto in Leo Generation (June 14, 1939 to August 19, 1957) – The Silent Generation (1925-1945) and Baby Boomers (1946-1964) express many of the behaviors assigned to this generation. The Pluto in Leo Generation were labeled "hippy, flower child and rock n roll generation" with their slogan being "Make Love Not War." Self-expressive, artistic, spiritual, confident are a few positive attributes of this generation. Metaphysical, new age and alterative spirituality were popular among this generation. Negative attributes of this generation include; arrogance, selfishness, superficiality and extravagance. Most of the world's debt, pollution and food issues are credited to this generation. Baby Boomers are often titled as the Narcissistic generation, being self-absorbed, having feelings of superiority, envious/jealous and lacking empathy. Leo rules the child archetype which is why most of this generation refuses to grow up. Inflated ego, pride and identity are problems this generation faced and continue to face. This generation seems to lack sense of community and structure. Gaining self-awareness and not evolving with such awareness. Many single parents came out of this generation. This generation couldn't bridge the gap between love of self and love of others. Social issues that contributed to the MEIs of this generation were:

-Civil Rights Movement

-Vietnam War & Anti-War Movement

-The Watergate Scandal

-Fight for Women's Rights

      The above social issues, contributed/created many traumas experienced by this generation thus deterring some from addressing many issues of self and propelling them into a whirlwind of social issues that continued to feed their own psychological problems.

Pluto in Virgo Generation (August 19, 1957 to October 5, 1971 | April 17, 1972 to July 30, 1972) – Generation X (1965 – 1981) populates Pluto in Virgo Generation. Generation X is often referred to as the "Neglected Middle Child" generation. The beginning of the large wave of "Indigo Children." The behavior of most middle children being rebellious, peacemakers, out of place/disjointed but make good friends and thrive on friendship. The Public Enemy song, Fight the Power, encapsulates Generation X. People born in the Pluto in Virgo generation have problems with control. This generation has problems with people in their lives controlling them whether it is family, friends or the government. Over analytical and over critical of themselves and others is another trait of the Generation Xer. Growing up in many single parent homes and being the generation of many divorced parents allowed this generation to seek comfort in friends. But, many Generation Xers took this to an unpleasant level by hiding their true nature and feelings around their "friends"; often thinking about what others may think. Positive attributes of Generation X are: overcoming society's expectations, love of self - becoming more aware of healthy eating, yoga and exercise; revolution in technology and activism came out of this generation. Generation X is less self-centered than the generation of their parents, Baby Boomers. Negative attributes of this generation are, feelings of inferiority, not feeling worthy, jealousy and low self-esteem. Social issues that contributed to the MEI's of this generation were:

-The War on Drugs

-Reaganomics

-The Crack Epidemic

-Gang Violence

Generation Y aka Millennials is a diverse generation. There aren't many calculated estimates on when this generation begins and ends. Most guess that Millennials were born in the late 70s/early 80s well into the mid 90s and early 2000s. The first half of millennials born in the 70s to mid 80s are governed by Pluto in Libra.

Pluto in Libra Generation (July 30, 1972 – November 5, 1983 | May 18, 1984 – August 27, 1984) Some Generation Xers are found be born with Pluto in Libra while the beginning of the millennial generation is being born into the world. Although every generation has their share of Indigo children, Pluto in Libra is the continued wave of Indigo children incarnating on earth. Libra is the sign of change and these millennials born with Pluto in Libra have changed many old norms of society. "Out with the Old, In with the New" is the motto of this generation. Millennials are even more rebellious than the generations before them. Going against and destroying anything that is not in balance with their own beliefs such as religion and government. Positive attributes of this generation are balance, self-love and harmony. Negative attributes include obsessed with compromise and trying to fix the errors of previous generations.

Pluto in Scorpio Generation (August 27, 1984 – January 17, 1995 | April 21, 1995 – November 10, 1995) The second wave of millennials populate is generational wave. The motto, "Respect is Earned Not Given" encapsulates this generation. Many born within Pluto in Scorpio are referred as "old souls" to those around them. Anger and questions about the world populate the minds of this generation. Many millennials under this generation are seen as "difficult" by parents and relatives. While Generation Xers were rebellious for rebellions sake, Millennials of Pluto in Scorpio are rebellious due to personal disdain for the world around them. Pluto in Scorpio

Generation are said to experience the ego death phenomenon known as "Dark Night of the Soul" at an early age. Symptoms of this phenomenon become active early in the lives of these individuals feeding feelings of depression, loneliness, confusion and frustration. This journey causes many to seek alternative spirituality. These individuals are often interested in the occult, death and metaphysics. Positive attributes of this generation are self-transformation, connection with the inner child, and self-healing. Negative attributes of this generation are feeling and remaining stuck (in one's head and emotions), and stubbornness. Many of the social issues of the 80s poured into the early and mid 90s, affect the MEI's of this generation.

Many social issues such as Jim Crow, slavery and other horrors have impacted many generations before the ones mentioned above. The generations after such traumatic social events have continued to harbor the same issues and repeat the same cycles and create new ones.

There are a few more generations after the ones listed above but for the sake of time I chose not to mention them. Information is available all over to find more information about these generations and others. This section was written to highlight the issues we all hold on to. Stemming from social problems that invade our personal lives. Remaining unaware of effects that many social issues had on us that fuels more of our personal issues must end. Good thing that it doesn't take much to reprogram your energy to dispel all the energy of others that have been feeding off your energy and causing you to remain vulnerable. You must set your intentions of breaking out of the cycle of repeated behaviors and thoughts and work towards this goal. With this intention programmed you already program yourself toward healing energies. You will then manifest people and/or events that will correspond with this goal and begin to stimulate energies that will release previous stagnant energy. Look at the above breakdown of societal issues that affect ones MEIs as a guide to not stay trapped in personal pitfalls given to you by others. You will not and should not try to remedy the issues of a generation. Acknowledge what has happened and move on. The woes of society, impact us all on a very personal level but now is the time to acknowledge what has happened to self and work towards exiling the traumas accumulated that reside within our energy centers.

Healing yourself by working to cleanse and balance your chakra will help to ease repressed and lingering emotions. Once you make the commitment to work on your own energy centers it opens the door that allows free-flowing transmissions between you, your ancestors and other entities. Balanced and clean chakras are vital for productive interaction with spirits especially ancestors. Clear chakras, aura and mindset/intentions are the best fundamentals you can have to create your own ancestral deity system.

STEP 1: BUILDING YOUR FOUNDATION

Now is the time to decide which ancestors you wish to work with. It can be anyone from your family tree and anyone you admire who isn't part of your family lineage that has now passed on. It doesn't matter if you knew them personally during their time in the physical, you will soon forge a connection that transcends boundaries set by humanity. You will be connecting with ancestors on a level that goes beyond all the psychological baggage their spirit has been bombarded with. You are in control of which spirits you want to commune with. Although there may be times when one of your ancestors may want to connect with you but you don't wish to – this is perfectly fine. That ancestor will just have to respect your decision. First you must decide who you wish to contact and connect with. Start small and then increase as you become more confident and familiar with communicating with spirits.

The way in which you can choose which ancestors to work with can vary. You can choose an uncle who you've never met but you've heard awesome stories about and because of this you think he's a cool guy. You can choose to contact your grandmother because she was always the nurturer of the family and you have fond memories of her. You could even choose the ancestor of someone completely remote from your family tree that you just have an extreme interest in. For example, I've been fascinated with the famous magician by the name of Black Herman. Although we're not related by blood, he is still an ancestor I admire and respect l and have worked with due to my interest in his history. The choice is yours on who you want to connect with.

Some of you may be thinking about the ancestors who've done a bit of wrong-doings or inexcusable acts during their time here on earth. Asking questions such as, should I contact them? What if they're trying to speak to me? Just like everything else in this guide the answer is simple – you have the power to choose if you wish to be bothered with a spirit or not. If you had a relative that abused you and you can't forgive or forget that incident – do not entertain these thoughts nor this spirit's energy. The reasons for creating your own ancestral deity system is to bring you healing, prosperity, wisdom and whatever else you desire. If you don't feel like you will get these things through contacting and connecting with ancestors who've hurt you then don't engage them and if they are engaging you just firmly stand your ground and tell them to leave you alone. Majority of the time these types of spirits will not try to contact you because they know you are not ready and most likely they are not ready. If you are being plagued by the spirit of someone who has done wrong to you in the past, more than likely you are manifesting and projecting unresolved feelings and issues buried deep within your subconscious and you should begin healing yourself emotionally before continuing further. If you have a few ancestors that you are eager to work with just know that they are even more eager to talk and connect with you.

Many of you who are reading this book are familiar with the routine way of dealing with ancestors, through traditional methods of worship/veneration. As your guide, I do not advise that you blindly worship anyone or thing. In the context of what I'm trying to convey in this book is that you should respect your ancestors as much as you respect yourself. They are not separate from you, they are not some external energy or entity you should fear or blindly appease out of fear. Your energy is their (ancestors) energy and vice versa. What you should have is a mutual love and understanding for them because they do for you. So, don't be anal about how you should speak to them. Converse with them in the manner you would a best friend or someone you love immensely. The rules of this physical world do not matter (pun intended) in the spirit world. Most of the rules given here on this plane are made and followed by people out of fear and ignorance. There is no need to be fearful or continue to remain in a state of ignorance. Gone should be the fear that they won't love, respect or listen to you because you didn't address them by a certain title or because you're not honoring them in some grandiose way. In any event that an ancestor or any spirit demand that you act out some sort of exaggerated ritual in their honor then you are clearly dealing with an extremely low level entity/thought-form; and should re-evaluate your intentions behind contacting your ancestors in addition to working out any mental, emotional and personal problems you've been neglecting. To attract/manifest this type of energy is a sign that you're at a low level in your spiritual and mental development to attract/manifest spirits that would come to you in this manner. One of the major things that allows us to encounter low energy is due to phony intentions.

Some people are on this spiritual quest just to validate themselves amongst their peers. These individuals are often lacking self-esteem and self-worth but project that they are better than others. Some just want to feel important. Other choose to begin spiritual connect to distract themselves from the problems in their life. Often the reason why some attract low spirits is because they are trying to learn spiritual knowledge for the sake of "one-upping" others. Others use it as a form of escapism – since they've been shunned by society at large or can't seem to "fit" in they turn to the world of spirit to appease those emotions, thus feeding the ego. This attitude is then carried throughout their journey and interactions within the spirit world thus having dire effects such as attracting low level energy and feeding neglected psychological problems. Just like some people, some spirits hold jealous and inferior feelings and are attracted to like emotions and energies.

Figuring out which ancestors you wish to contact is the crucial first step in creating your ancestral deity system. Once you've made up your mind about which ancestors you wish to empower and connect with – now it's time to gather as much physical information about them that is possible. Physical information such as; birth and death dates, favorite food, liquor, music, etc. Anything that you can gather you need to catalog it in a notebook (or the note section in the back of this book) designed to chronicle your ancestor work. By knowing what they enjoyed while living will be what you place on your ancestor altar. It will also be some of the objects you can use to feed/empower them with more energy. I'll elaborate more on empowering, feeding and what to include on your ancestor altar in step 2. For now, try to recall fond memories of them and incidents that may have occurred that you think was their attempt at contacting you.

The sky's the limit on how many ancestors you can add to your ancestral deity system but I would advise you to start small (one or two) and work your way up so you don't overwhelm yourself.

STEP 2: CREATING YOUR ANCESTOR ALTAR

Your Ancestor Altar is your base of operations. Anything that belonged or reminds you of your beloved ancestors can be placed here. General items that are beneficial for every ancestor altar are:

- Florida Water
- One Pink or Blue 7 Day Candle
- Joss Paper
- A Glass of Water
- Frankincense and Myrrh Incense
- Kananga Water
- A Shot of Rum (or any alcohol of your choice)
- A Meal of your Choice
- A Table to Set Up Your Altar
- Photos of Ancestors
- Any Items that Reminds You of Your Ancestors

Florida Water

The Florida Water is used to cleanse your altar and the surrounding area of any negative energies. It's a great opening offering to your ancestral spirits because it calms the energy of an environment in addition to allowing clear communication. It also builds and strengthens the protective vibrations of your home. You can place a glass of Florida Water on your altar or you can place it in a spray bottle and spritz your altar and the entire room where your altar is located. Florida water removes emotions/energies such as anger, sadness, and depression thus allowing room for the emotions of love, luck, and prosperity.

Florida Water can be found online or at your local Spiritual Botanica. Make sure to buy at least two to three bottles because if you're spiritually cleansing your altar and environment at daily, weekly or monthly – this stuff will disappear fast.

7 Day Candle

Traditionally, people tend to use a white candle on their altar because the vibration that a white candle emits is that of harmony, protection and healing. A white candle is excellent to place on your ancestor altar or any altar. I use a blue candle because blue symbolizes water. Water being a great conductor of spiritual energy. It symbolizes the emotions, enticing one to be more expressive; as well as promoting healing energy – cleansing the mind, body and spirit. Blue candles also promote joy, harmony and guidance. The planet Saturn also corresponds with blue. Saturn is known as the planet of death. Signifying the end of what is 'known' and transcending. Much like the act of communicating with the dead; what was previously known was that death was final but now through our attempts at communicating with spirits we have transcended those previous beliefs. Saturn corresponds with the sphere Binah on Tree of Life and Satariel on the Qlipothic Tree.

Pink is the universal color of happiness and love; the exact type of energy you want to invoke within yourself, your environment and within your ancestors. The heart chakra also resonates with pink; it is the gateway where the energy of the physical realm and spiritual realm meet. This is the middle ground where initial contact with the spiritual world can develop. Compassion, forgiveness and trust are some of the many emotions that radiate from the heart chakra. Balancing the heart chakra is the first step of creating a solid foundation to connect with ancestors and other spirits.

You can choose any color you like but from my own experience I enjoy the vibrations emitted from the colors blue or pink. When you first create your altar, I recommend allowing the candle to burn out completely and even getting a few more candles to light continuously to help build up much needed energy to really get the ball rolling.

The duration that these 7-day candles will burn varies on the energy. From my experience, I'll get a good 4 days out of these candles before lighting another one. Walmart usually sells 7-day candles in select colors. Again, you can find these candles in bulk online or at a Spiritual Botanica.

Joss Paper

In Asian cultures, it is customary to burn spirit money aka Joss Paper (Joss means lucky). As stated in the section detailing Ancestor Worship in China – the purpose behind burning spirit money is to help your ancestors in the afterlife. It is believed (in China) that your ancestors want to enjoy the same luxuries they had in their physical life. This is a cool belief and idea – but with my own personal journey into the realm of the ancestors I've remixed the original meaning behind burning Joss Paper to fit my own disposition. I burn Joss Paper for my ancestors as another way to empower them. Since this book is written within the context of our beloved ancestors being powerful chaos beings – the burning of Joss Paper is an offering to them to continue to empower their primal power. Just as flowers and fruits as offered to widely celebrated entities; Florida Water, Candles, Joss Paper and other items serve the same purpose for your ancestors.

Joss Paper can be purchased online or at any Asian Market. In addition to your Joss Paper you should purchase a fire proof bowl or plate to place your Joss Paper in once you ignite it.

A Glass of Water

The act of getting a glass of water for someone to drink is something we all do out of respect for those we care about. Your ancestors will feed off the essence of the nice fresh water you serve them. Water is alive and can carry many vibrations and frequencies. Water can be programmed though visualization, images, thoughts, music and words. The basic vibration you are emitting to the water is one of love, power and admiration for your ancestors. Everything you are placing on their altar is to empower them – so the vibration that the water will carry is of power, respect and unity.

A rule of thumb to follow is to serve any type of water you would drink yourself. Any type of water will do honestly. I generally serve spring water since it comes from a natural source and tends to be free of any harmful chemicals that may carry negative vibrations.

Frankincense and Myrrh Incense

Frankincense and Myrrh has many spiritual benefits. Producing positive vibrations, protecting and strengthening the body and spirit. The Ancient Egyptians used frankincense to help guide the soul through the gates of the afterlife. Myrrh keeps negative entities away and adds more power to supportive and compassionate spirits.

Copal is another fragrance that attracts benevolent spirits and is often burned during the celebration of the dead. Copal helps to elevate your mood and surroundings and clears blockages of any kind. Traditionally it was used as an offering to deities. Seems to be a fitting gift for your ancestors.

There are tons and tons of incenses, essential oils, perfumes, etc. that you can use. Whatever fragrance you deem worthy of placing and burning on your ancestor altar is suitable, just go with your intuition.

Kananga Water

Kananga water is a type of floral water often used in Hoodoo. It's an item often used in spiritual rituals for purification and contacting the dead. It is widely believed that the spirits of our ancestors enjoy the scent of Kananga water making it a great item used when conjuring them. It has a very pleasing spicy sweet scent. Some of the ingredients of Kananga water include ylang-ylang, cinnamon and almond. Analyzing these ingredients gives a bit on insight into why this is an awesome floral water to use for ancestor work.

Ylang-ylang offers protection and banishes negativity, soothing the mind and emotions. Cinnamon is universally used for abundance, love, happiness and protection. Almond attracts prosperity, luck and love.

Using Kananga water is simple, you just add a few drops of it to a bowl of clean water and place it onto your ancestor altar. The vibrations emitted from Kananga water programs your surroundings and sending positive signals to any spirits around you. Any religious supply store will carry Kananga Water.

A Shot of Rum

For spiritual purposes, ancient civilizations have always used alcohol and other substances to temporarily eliminate analytical thinking, isolate the ego in hopes of elevating consciousness, changing their thoughts, feelings and perception. Indigenous cultures around the world believed that spirits were always involved in the lives of the living. Alcohol alters the consciousness of those who consume it making it the perfect vessel to merge the spiritual and physical worlds. Think of it as one of the many alternatives such as meditation, fasting, cannabis, etc. that are used to alter one's mind to cause a spiritual revelation.

I chose Rum since it has a strong connection to the ancestors from Africa and parts of the Caribbean who cultivated and manufactured it. Use whatever alcohol you enjoy because if you like it, your ancestors will enjoy it as well. A shot glass is only recommended to make things easier than pouring libations because you won't have to pour libations every day. Just fill the shot glass up with the spirit of your choice and place it on your ancestor altar and done! Just like all things in the universe, alcohol has an essence, a spirit – your ancestors feed off this essence. Just as vitamins and minerals aid the human body, alcohol acts in a similar manner; giving power, healing and prosperity to our beloved ancestors.

A Meal of Your Choice

Serving an ancestor any meal of your choice is another way to give them energy and appease their spirit. You can also serve them any meal they enjoyed when they were in the physical realm. Just as I stated before, everything in the universe has a spirit and your ancestors can feed off the essence/spirit of the food, beverages and other items you choose to serve them. In many books that deal with ancestor worship, they state that it isn't good for one ancestors to consume any food with salt because it makes the food unpalatable. I chose to go with my gut, and the method that I used that yielded results was to serve my ancestors food in the same manner I would serve it to them if they were still in the physical realm. My older brother Zandor loved homemade French fries; I prepared the French fries the same way he cooked them while he was living, adding sea salt and garlic powder.

After placing them onto my altar and then channeling him to communicate with him to see if he enjoyed what I had prepared – his answer was absolutely. I then proceeded to ask him would it matter if I put salt and other seasonings on the fries. He said, yes; I then asked why, and the gist of his response was, "why would he eat his French fries any other way?" So, why would you or those you care about want something that isn't good or appetizing? What would be the point in consuming something if it is something you don't want nor enjoy? Most of the time your ancestors can and will be just as picky with their food as if they were still in a physical body. Just go with your gut, you will know what food to serve them. One rule I follow when serving food to my ancestors, is to serve them food in the same quality that I would enjoy it. For example, I'm against using regular iodize salt, instead I prefer sea salt or pink Himalayan salt. Also, I don't serve them tap water, instead I choose spring water. It's just best to go with what you feel to be right. Again, if you wouldn't eat it why would you serve it to someone you love unless it's a specific dish they enjoy and you don't. Just go with your intuition and if in doubt just ask your ancestor what they would like once you begin to communicate with them which can be found in Step 4.

Since you are setting up your altar and preparing to dive into the world of the ancestors just go with a neutral meal; such as a family favorite or something that would be served during the holiday in your household.

A Table to Set-Up Your Altar

Trees resonate with powerful, ancient and wise energy. In various African cultures trees served, *"to establish and sustain a sense of community, to communicate with ancestors, to connect to a deity, or to symbolize place."* You can find more wonderful information on the magic of trees in Stephanie Rose Bird's book, <u>A Healing Grove: African Tree Remedies and Rituals for the Body and Spirit</u>. Trees also act as a physical metaphor for the various dimensions that are commonplace in dealing with spirits, deities and ancestors. The roots of a tree represent the physical world, third dimension or planet earth. The base/trunk of the tree symbolizes the middle world such as the astral plane and the branches of the tree represent heaven. If looking from another perspective, the roots can represent the Qlippoth, which is the "dark" side of the Tree of Life; while the growth of the tree represents the Tree of Life and its various realms of consciousness illustrated as the 11 spheres. These realms are made official due to the power of the Qlippoth also known as the underworld/ancestor realm.

Trees have the power to animate life, transform energy and allow communication with deities, entities and spirits; making it a perfect vessel to use as the base for your altar. A wooden table is perfect to place any objects deemed worthy for your altar; the same energy housed in the trees that make the table will be present in your altar. There are so many places where you can purchase a wooden table so the options are endless. One of the best things you can do is buy a used or antique table since these types of objects have history and character.

Photos of Your Ancestors

Not much to be explained here other than to place photos of your ancestors on your altar either in frames or on the wall behind your altar. The photos can be of anyone you deem worthy enough to connect with. You can include photos of your genetic ancestors whether you knew them or not; you can also include photos of people that are not related to you by blood. It is not taboo in this system to have a picture of J. Dilla next you a photo of your beloved grandfather.

Do whatever you feel is right. Know that you are not obligated to honor or contact anyone you don't want to. Pictures of these individuals have no place on your altar. Any photos you pick of your ancestors act as a reminder and indicator of who you are programming your altar to feed and energize.

Any Items that Reminds You of Your Ancestors

You can place anything you deem worthy of adding to your altar. Let your imagination run wild. Think about one of your favorite aunt's that you are now planning to connect with. Sit back and reflect. Did she remind you of someone or something? Maybe she had a laid-back disposition almost Buddha like. Suddenly, your mind jumps from her to the image of Buddha and you begin to see the similarities between your favorite aunt and Buddha. You then begin to identify her as a female Buddha figure, but your imagination doesn't stop there. Memories of her favorite color green start to arise in your mind which is green. Green and a Buddha like attitude can be associated with the Goddess Tara. Looking back at your thought process, you just went through from favorite aunt, cool/calm mentality, Buddha, green and finally the Goddess Tara.

Now, behold when you rummage through some of her favorite belongings you find a dish she cherished that she may have used as a candy dish or maybe you find that she collected figurines from Asia and one figurine calls out to you. These are the items you would place on your ancestor altar. But don't stop here, you could be shopping at the store and see something that reminds you of an ancestor, make sure to place it on your altar. The feeling you get when you see, hear or think about something that reminds you of an ancestor is one of the many ways our ancestors communicate with us. This is one way you can connect mythology with your ancestors. In Step 6, I will go into greater detail about crafting a personal mythology for your ancestors. Here is a bit of my own personal experience with crafting a mythology for my own ancestor – my brother Zandor.

The Zandoric Realm

My descent into the realm of the ancestors came after I moved to New Orleans and engrossed myself into New Orleans Voodoo as well as Hoodoo. I studied and read many books on both subjects before getting bored. Then I turned my attention to communicating with the dead. At the time, I was researching with my friend, Sean, about the afterlife and how to communicate with the dead. During my time of reading and studying everything I could about the afterlife and death, memories of my older brother resurfaced. His laugh, smile, favorite food and activities popped up in my head so much that I couldn't shake them. If my mind wandered to something else it soon went back to thinking about my brother.

Along with the constant thoughts on my brother, I kept hearing Mushu's opening monologue from Disney's Mulan. The exact words I kept hearing over and over in my head were, *"I live! Now, tell me what mortal needs my protection great ancestor, you just say the word and I'm there."* I'm a huge Disney fan, I've watched most of their animated movies countless times – so this act of something random like a line or song from a Disney movie popping in my head is far from abnormal. I'm known to break out in sporadic Disney songs, acting them out, from start to finish. Since I couldn't shake this phrase from my mind. I decided to seek the advice of my friend Sean. I told him how I kept hearing the same line repeatedly in my head from Mulan and how Mulan is one of my favorite Disney movies. He suggested I watch Mulan and mentioned that spirits make contact in subtle ways. He was sure that it was spiritual contact.

Without hesitation, I signed into my Netflix account and began watching Mulan. I watched this movie hundreds of time but this time was different, I noticed things I never did before. Through Mulan's quest to fight for her father she summoned the help of her ancestors. The fact that the movie deals with ancestors made my mind race. The ancestors have always been part of the movie but because my perception is broader, the role of the ancestors caught my attention big time. Other things about the movie started to pop out to me. Mushu, the fact that he is a red dragon; Mushu is voiced by Eddie Murphy and the fact that he is Mulan's companion/driving force/protector. I suddenly had an epiphany. I connected Zandor with Mushu. The similarities between Mushu's voice actor (Eddie Murphy) and my brother Zandor are uncanny. They share the same complexion, same height and both are funny as hell. Mushu is a red dragon, red represents power, passion and love while dragon represents strength, magic, protection and wisdom. I now saw these as traits of my brother both on earth and now in the afterlife.

Moving onto parts of Mushu's dialogue throughout the movie that spoke to me.

(1) I live! So, tell me what mortal needs my protection Great Ancestor. You just say the word and I'm there…Anybody who's foolish enough to threaten our family; vengeance will be mine!

(2) Who am I? Who am I? I am the guardian of lost souls! I am the powerful, the pleasurable, the indestructible Mushu.

(3) My powers are beyond your mortal imagination. For instance, my eyes can see straight through your armor.

These quotes stood out to me, when hearing them I got a rush of energy, I could feel a pull in my heart center and solar plexus. The words of Mushu that resonated with me reflected what my brother was trying to illustrate to me. His power and nature was being expressed by the lines of Mushu in the movie. I went back to my notes about voodoo that I'd written some time ago. Mushu is a red dragon, sometime ago I became familiar with the Petro spirits. Within this group of spirits is a spirit by the name of Ti-Jean Zandor also known as Prince Zandor; who is said to be a deity of conversation and gossip. Prince Zandor is often depicted as a short man in red who devours people. Another petro spirit goes by the name of Ti-Jean Dantor who is carefree spirit that enjoys women and parties. Ti-Jean Petro is another aspect of this energy. He is a masculine force/energy, a spirit of fire and was one of the many driving force behind the Haitian Revolution. The word/name Zandor can be used interchangeably with Dantor and corresponds with voodoo entities such as Erzulie Dantor. Seeing so many versions of my beloved brother's name be used in a recognized spiritual system was a step in the right direction. It allowed me to begin associating his power with the power of pre-existing entities.

Ti-Jean Petro is the energy I connected with Mushu from Mulan since Mushu could produce fire, he protected Mulan and was one of the forces behind her pursuit for victory. I was able to connect some traits with my brother Zandor and Ti-Jean Petro including his favorite color - red, his enjoyment of spicy food, and his hothead attitude at times. Looking for more research about the name Zandor and its connection with voodoo, I found a book titled, Vodou Quantum Leap by Reginald Crosley. Along with reading this book I couldn't wait any longer and decided to contact my brother in the afterlife. I hoped on my Ouija board and began to channel him. (In Step 4, there is detailed information about channeling and other methods you can use to contact your ancestors.) The results were a success, I discovered many of his attributes that I would associate with a god. Such as his primal name, his powers and other various attributes. He told me the image that is great to represent his energy which is a red dragon. Ding-ding-ding! Mushu is a dragon. This really got me rolling because I was indeed experiencing a spiritual breakthrough and communicating with a loved one who was communicating back.

Red was Zandor's favorite color on earth but while channeling him he told me that maroon is a color he enjoys. Maroon is a variation of the color red. Reading Crosley's book, he talks about the Maroon people – who were African people who escaped slavery and formed settlements. According to Crosley, the Maroon people were familiar with the *"shadowy alternate realities"* which he refers to as Zandorism. Crosley then goes on to mention, *"The core of their rituals is the Petro Zandor rite. The vodouns or guards served in this rite are the most brutal and dangerous ones. Among them are: Ti-Jean Petro, Ti-Jean Zandor…"*

He goes on to mention more but I just decided to mention Petro and Zandor to demonstrate yet another connection to the information previously mentioned above. Not only is Maroon one way to identify him but it also gives further perspective of his energy, power and symbolism. All of this puts into perspective how the oldest people on planet earth i.e. indigenous people aka black people are primal, otherworldly, chaos beings. After discovering this bit of information about my beloved brother there was no room for doubt in my mind that not only is he a chaos being but so am I.

After gathering and digesting all the new information I had gathered about my brother and his power. The final link was made. Mushu acts as a gateway entity for Mulan between the other ancestors. My brother Zandor has been a gateway entity for me and my other ancestors whom I've been in contact with. Mushu was the guardian that awakened the ancestors, exactly like what my brother is doing for me and other ancestors as we connect with each other. Now, you may be asking; "How the fuck did you get all this from watching Mulan?!"

Simple questions with a simple answer. I'm communicating with my ancestor, someone who has my best interest at heart, someone who has lived with me, grown with me and continues to watch over me in the afterlife. A person who knows me probably better than I know myself making him the best candidate to know how to communicate and connect with me through my own interest. My brother Zandor knows I love Disney, has watched Disney movies with me during his time here on earth and continues to watch over me. It would only be natural to use my hobbies and interests as a tool to open the door of communication. We all have hobbies and interests and our friends, family and ancestors would be the best candidates to know our interests and how to use them to communicate with us. Don't just take my experience as the only way in which your ancestors can communicate with you, there is no limit but I will say that the easiest way to open the lines of communication would be through activities you are enthusiastic about. You may be interested in a type of music, you may suddenly get the urge to listen to a certain artist and song; within that song you may notice a few lyrics pop out to you and speak to you in a way it hasn't before, all correlating with your ancestral work. Don't limit yourself nor your ancestors. Trust yourself and follow your intuition, you have the power.

On a final note don't worry about matching tons of physical characteristics between an ancestors and entity/deity. It will not make or break your progress, it is only a means of helping you identify and understand your ancestors' primal energy. Be aware that you will feel doubt and second guess yourself. But that is perfectly normal. It is just your ego trying to hate on you and regain some control and halt your imagination. Just stay calm and remain confident in whatever messages and information you receive that uplifts and empowers you.

But, don't stop just because you found a link between the Goddess Tara and your favorite aunt. This doesn't mean you should worship the Goddess Tara as your aunt and vice versa. Think of the Gods and Goddesses of all the spiritual pantheons around the world as energy symbols. As symbols their primary purpose is to remind you of the primal power you hold within yourself not only as a temporary physical entity but beyond the constraints of humanity. Isis, Shiva, Freya and any other god or goddess from other cultures were created to illustrate this fact. The goal being to remember your cosmic place in the universe. A constant reminder of who you really are, greater than any god or goddess. You have many forms, numerous attributes, always changing, anything and everything resides within you.

STEP 3: SETTING THE TONE

Before you begin building your ancestor altar, you must first cleanse your home/apartment and your body. Supplies needed are:

- Spiritual Floor Bath: I recommend Creolin, it can be purchased at your local spiritual supply store. If you don't wish to use Creolin you can always make your own or buy something you deem suitable. A recipe I use from time to time is just some sea salt mixed with apple cider vinegar and water. I then mop all my floors with this mixture and wipe down my windows and door knobs to remove all negative energies.

- Spiritual Bath/Wash: These are two baths I used during the start of my spiritual journey which I recommend greatly if you have never done any type of spiritual cleansing. Fresh Bitter and Fresh Sweet herb baths are awesome. These can be purchased again at any spiritual supply store. You take the bitter bath first to remove all negativity and evil followed by the sweet bath that brings in prosperity, success and luck.

- Florida Water: Will be used to spray each corner of every room in your home/apartment. This nullifies and removes any stagnant energy that has been resting in the corners of your home. Alternatively, you can use sea salt and sprinkle this in the corners of every room.

- White Candle: It can be a 7-day jar candle or a tea light candle, it really doesn't matter. What does matter is your intention behind burning the candle, that intention being to purify your environment. Place the candle in the area you're choosing to place your ancestor altar.

- Music: Any type will do preferably something you enjoy or you know your ancestors will enjoy such as Michael Jackson, Sade, Earth Wind & Fire, Stevie Wonder, etc.; there are no limits. You don't have use the traditional music associated with spiritual work such as OM chants or drumming although you can by all means – do what you feel is right. Put something on that makes you feel good, this helps to cleanse the environment. Upbeat music uplifts the environment. Also, you're beginning to communicate with your ancestors so make it a huge event. Music is the introductory stage of any great event. Have fun, no spiritual work should be boring or feel like a chore.

Now is the time to put your music on, set your intention while lighting your candle, ready your mop and get to cleansing your home. After you're finished cleansing your environment, hop right into the tub and begin your spiritual bath. After everything is completed it is time to begin erecting your ancestor altar!

Gather all the supplies given in Step Two, it's now time to begin arranging your ancestor altar in whatever manner you deem appropriate. Before you place anything on the surface you've choosen to house your altar, go and grab your Florida Water. Pour some of the Florida water onto a rag and wipe down the table, wiping everywhere. The purpose behind doing this is to cleanse it of negative energy and dirt.

First thing to place on your altar are the pictures of your ancestors placing them either on the wall behind the altar or inside picture frames on top of your altar. This is an exciting first step, the photos act as a conduit allowing you to focus and center your intention which is to gather the energy of your ancestors. You may sense your ancestors' presence during the construction and decoration of your altar - as if you all are creating the altar together. Once you place all the photos on your altar, now begin placing any special items you selected. Such as any statues and personal items from a favorite handkerchief to flowers to whatever you deem appropriate. Next, gather your glass of fresh water, a bowl of cold water along with the Kananga water, a bottle of rum or liquor of your choice and begin setting everything up. Place the glass of fresh water wherever on your altar followed by the bowl of water and add a splash of Kananga to fragrance the water. Finally placing the bottle of liquor wherever you like but hold off on pouring some in a small shot glass because this will come later during the welcoming ceremony. Grab your pink or blue 7-day candle, joss paper, and incense. Load the incense holder with the scent of your choice, gather a fireproof bowl for your joss paper and place the candle in the center of your altar. Lastly grab whatever meal you've prepared for yourself and your ancestors and place it on to your altar. Now it is time to begin the welcoming ceremony. Set your intention saying it aloud then light your candle followed by your incense and begin to pour your liquor into the shot glass. Now you will recite an invocation. I adapted the invocation below from the book, <u>Ancestors: Hidden Hands, Healing Spirits for your Use and Empowerment</u> by Ra Ifagbemi Babalawo. You can use the invocation in this book to create your own or modify it in any manner of your preference.

Ancestor Invocation

Facing your ancestor altar, begin to say:

I praise the Great Mother of All, Supreme, Divine, Omnipotent and in all things.

I praise my higher-self for guiding me on my spiritual journey and protecting me through countless lifetimes.

I praise all my Great and Noble ancestors who have traveled the path of eternal love and self-realization.

I praise all my indigenous ancestors across the globe.

I praise all the ancestral spirits who have died in the harsh conditions bestowed by humanity.

I praise all ancestors known and unknown.

I praise... (Say the full name of each ancestor whose picture you have placed on the altar.)

Spirits welcome to my humble honoring. May this flame bring you light and power. May the water refresh your spirits. May this food and drink whose spiritual essence you eat cause you to grow strong so that you will not have to beg for energy or wither. Know that you are special among the spirits because you have descendants who honor you and will not let you be forgotten. Oh, Great Spirit family, since you are free of body and form, we know that you now have greater wisdom and power. Continue to protect (say your name). *Use your greater power and influence to help....* (say whatever it is you may need or want assistance with such as health, finances, protection, knowledge, etc.)

After you're finished this invocation you may feel a presence. This presence belongs to your ancestors, welcome them and enjoy the reunion. The presence may come as a feeling, idea, thought, smell, memory – be open to however it chooses to come to you. The ancestor invocation is followed by your ancestor statement. In your statement, you will express your own thoughts, feelings and intentions for beginning ancestor communication. Here is my own statement I used during my ceremony, again tweak it however you wish.

Ancestor Statement

As you already know I am into magick and the occult, which means I'm interested in talking to spirits, performing rituals and participating in alternate forms of spirituality. I've decided to honor you and create this altar, not only to honor you and supply you with energy but to also empower myself and fuel my spiritual journey. By honoring you, I give you energy and power and in return I receive it from you. With this energy and power, I wish for you to remember who you truly are. What I mean by who you truly are I mean your primal self, your soul name, who you truly are, before any of lifetimes you've experienced. Please supply me with wisdom and protection. Lastly, do not expect me to use your energy nor my own to communicate, contact or help any of our relatives. You have seen how lost these individuals are. I will not take it upon myself to help these individuals, they are not my priority. My only concern lays with my

64

spiritual plight, raising myself up as well as making sure my physical needs are taken care of and run smoothly so that I can continue to grow spiritually and feed your energy. Please feel free to use the energy given to you in the form of liquor, food, money (joss paper), music and words to help those family members and friends you wish to help.

Congratulations! You have taken the first steps toward completing your ancestral deity system. Now the door of communication is wide open!

STEP 4: MAKING CONTACT

There are many ways that our ancestors choose to communicate with us. This step will explain effective forms of communication that you can embark on to contact the spirit world. One of the first forms of communication you can begin using right now is to talk aloud as if your ancestors are physically present in the room with you. Talk about anything you'd like such as television shows, movies, work/school, relationships, dreams, anything. The more you do this, the more you will feel the presence of your ancestors. Just because you can't physically see them anymore doesn't mean they aren't with you. They are always with you and have been with you before you even became aware of their presence. If you're having trouble talking aloud just think back when you were a child and you may have had an imaginary friend. Your critical, waking mind couldn't do much to interfere with your imagination as a child because you believed your imagination to be real. Make the effort to apply yourself, form a connection and use the power of your divine mind by exercising your imagination in this way. When you first start talking aloud it may feel weird and you may feel silly. But keep doing it.

Eventually, you will notice that you will feel the presence of those ancestors you are communicating with and soon you will even begin to get responses in the form of thoughts outside of your own. You will feel how genuine the responses you receive will be. This is how you exercise your clairaudient ability. Clairaudience means 'clear hearing' and it is a psychic ability that allows you to perceive sounds and voices from the spirit world. Clairaudience usually occurs in the form of thoughts coming from inside the head (sometimes you may hear voices physically but not always). You will know the difference between your own thoughts and that of someone else. It is important to do a lot of energy work on yourself in the form of clearing your aura and balancing your chakras so you will have a system put into place to know when you are receiving foreign thoughts and feelings. Practice talking aloud whenever you can; this also helps to balance your throat chakra which is the center where clairaudience is developed. You will become more comfortable receiving spiritual contact and become familiar with feeling the presence of your ancestors.

When you first begin communicating with your ancestors, it can be emotionally taxing. Just by performing the exercise above you may have opened the flood gates on many emotions you thought were resolved. Please take as much time as you need. Continue to talk to your ancestors about how you feel and what your plans are with creating your ancestral deity system. Please move on whenever you're ready.

Ouija Board

The next form of communication will begin with the Ouija board. Using one will further thrust you into the world of spirit. This method of full blown spiritual contact will help to ease those doubts that may continue to pop up about the validity of the spirit world, your ancestors and the power of your imagination.

When you begin to use a spirit board you may get a light day-dreamy feeling. This is alpha state; which occurs during meditation, napping, dreaming and visualization. You may also notice a few ways in which the answers to your questions will arise. Inside your own head, you may hear the answer to your question before the physical response is given through the plachette. This is your clairaudient ability at work. The usual way you will receive answers on the spirit board will be through the movement of the plachette. When you begin to ask for answers such as the primal names of your ancestors, the names will be strange and sometimes won't be English friendly but look at the names of other deities/entities/spirits. Some of the names given, correspond with the language associated with the culture attached to the deity but sometimes the names are completely foreign and don't even seem to correspond with anything on Earth such as the names of angels, demons and various spirits. Don't worry if you have trouble understanding or pronouncing the primal names you receive from your ancestors.

Now, before you decide to get your spirit board out, decide which ancestor you are going to contact then grab a piece of paper and a pen. Write some questions you want to ask the ancestor you've chosen to talk to. Keep the questions short. You want to ask questions that will validate you are speaking with the right spirit; such as: birthday, date of death, nicknames, favorite food/drink, etc. Build your questions around information that can be verified. You can verify the questions if you know the answers to them or you can call and talk to a living relative who will know the answers to such questions to get validation. Once you've gathered your questions, make sure that your environment is cleansed, go and grab that Florida water and spray some in each corner of the room and a little wouldn't hurt to spray on the Ouija board too. Set up your Ouija board and candle on a table or on the floor, wherever you are comfortable with. Make sure the room is quiet and free from distractions. Place your spirit board in front of you and the candle out of reach so that you don't bump it. I personally prefer to use my spirit board in a room only illuminated by candle light which helps me to get into alpha state quicker. You can use more than one candle if you're using your board in a dark room, if not just one candle will do. As a tool to help focus your mind and raise the vibration of the room - begin to relax and meditate for a bit. You can count your breath or simply slow your breathing. Looking at the candle flame is good too. After a minute or so, you can do a quick aura protection visualization by just imagining yourself with a protective barrier around you and nothing negative can get through this shield. Then call on your spirit guide, HGA (holy guardian angel) or any spirit ally you've worked with and trust.

Address the spirit by name followed by the intent of this meeting. Tell your spirit guide which ancestor you are trying to reach. Meditate on the name of the ancestor you wish to communicate with. Using the flame of the candle, focus on its movement and try to limit the times you blink to help induce a light trance-like state, relaxing your mind and body further. After a few minutes of meditation, place the tip of your fingers on the plachette. The placement of your fingers isn't important just remain relaxed. You must be relaxed to feel the energy around you and the subtle movement of the plachette. Now you're ready to breach the veil between worlds.

Start by stating the full name of the ancestor you are trying to talk to, followed by asking the question, "Is (name of ancestor) here?" At first you may not receive any response but continue to ask. If you don't get any answers you need to take a break and come back another time. At first the plachette will move slightly but stay calm and focused. Relax your body, especially your hands. Make sure you're not pressing the plachette onto the board creating resistance. Eventually the plachette will move all on its own! Continue to focus and remain calm until you get results. Once you notice that the plachette is moving all on its own and you are receiving answers from your ancestor – you may get emotional. This is okay, just remain calm. After you've gathered answers to the questions you prepared earlier, conclude the session with thank you, I love you or whatever you feel is appropriate.

After clearing the area of all the materials used during this session, you're now tasked with verifying the information given to you by your ancestor. Getting answers to these simple questions will help to convince yourself about the existence of life after death and that your ancestors were communicating with you. It also helps to ease tension and fear. After verifying the information given, you can move on to ask other questions about how they are in the afterlife or what they've been up to all this time. The responses from your ancestor should and will be positive and loving. The energy you sense around you should be light and joyous. If you sense any low or heavy energy or receive any negative messages, end your session immediately. If all the steps and precautions were followed and you continue to attract low entities and energy then cleansing the environment again or changing anything about your altar won't do anything.

It is your thinking that is hindering you. Perhaps you have negative opinions about Ouija boards that you need to dismiss. What is shown to you in movies, television shows and internet videos are extremely exaggerated. You are using your Ouija board to connect with beloved ancestors, not to talk to strangers in the spiritual realms. The spirit world is vast and many entities reside there. Just as you can encounter a negative person on the street, you can encounter a negative entity in the spirit realm. You are dealing with the realm of the ancestors, a realm of complete love. If your mind and heart are unburdened and your intentions are clear then no problems will arise. If you continue to run into complications you should begin reprogramming your perception of the afterlife, ghosts and anything else associated with spirits. Your thinking has a huge impact on your spiritual work. No entity is out to harm you. If you think something is trying to harm you then ask yourself this question. "Why would someone who is not restricted by a physical body and free of all the woes of humanity, from debt to breakups want to bother me?" Or even ponder this question for a bit, "Is being a human the highest thing in the universe? Is my human existence and day to day life so important that some entity from some far part of the universe wants to take my human existence away from me?" Seriously think about it! Humanity is only temporary while your soul is eternal. Spirits are free to travel to various dimensions and engage with life in other worlds but they rather waste their time trying to harm you? It's silly to think that something out there in the universe is trying to harm and hinder you. You have tons of spiritual protection. Your spirit guides, deities and ancestors are always in your corner assisting you in your journey. They are forever by your side. Now is the time to harness your ancestral energy and empower yourself!

It takes no time to tune in and receive contact from your ancestors using a spirit board, making it extremely effective in building your ancestral deity system. As easy as it is to begin communicating with the beloved dead you may be forced to slow down while contacting your ancestors. Emotions, whether they're old and unresolved or buried will arise at first. It is perfectly normal to cry or be anxious. You are communicating with someone you loved that has passed on and although you may have thought you sorted out those feelings about your beloved ancestor or the dead and spirits altogether. Nothing can prepare you for the reunion of the feeling/energy of your loved one's presence again.

Meditation

Meditation is a simple method to use to begin channeling spirits. All you need are clear intentions and a quiet space to rest while you adventure through the subtle realms. Sit or lay down in a comfortable position and close your eyes. Take a few deep breaths and then begin to think of a mantra. OM is a common mantra used to induce the trance state that is great for channeling. You just want to repeat this mantra while relaxing. The mantra helps to tune your frequency to a higher vibration and distract your waking mind to hush all that mindless chatter we all experience.

Flame meditation and guided meditation are forms of meditation you can use to begin channeling your ancestors. Flame meditation is easy, all you need is a candle and a dark room. Place the candle on a table or some surface where the candle can be placed at eye level. Light the candle and turn the lights off or dim them. Get into a comfortable position where you can be idle for an extended amount of time. Focus on the candle flame while inhaling and exhaling slowly. You don't have to stare directly into the candle flame, adjust your eyes to look slightly downward, below the flame or even past the flame. After a few minutes of focusing on the flame, close your eyes. With your eyes closed you should be able to see the imprint of the candle flame. With your eyes still closed move your eyelids upward. This should make the imprint of the flame move as well. Adjust the imprint of the flame until it sits where your third eye is located (right between your brows). Rest the imprint of the candle there and focus on the imprint. Doing this activates the third eye and invites images from spirits. You can imagine yourself walking into the imprint which helps to focus your mind. You can call on your spirit guide to help in communicating with your ancestors.

Visualizing is great at this point, see yourself at your childhood home, communicating with the ancestor of your choice or see yourself walking in the forest trying to find your ancestors. You can even begin to think of questions you want to ask them and you may receive a response in the form of thoughts in the voice of your ancestor or your own but the answer is not something you could've thought of. You may receive images of things, people and objects; which are ways spirits choose to communicate. It will look just like a movie or images that pop into your mind via your imagination.

With guided meditation, you can listen to any meditation you're comfortable with. Many guided meditations can be found on YouTube. Creating your own guided meditation is also an option. Below is a sample script you can use to craft your own self-guided meditation. Make sure to grab a recorder and record yourself reciting the script so you can play it back during your meditation.

Sample Guided Meditation Script

I am slowly going into a state of deep relaxation. Slowly and surely, my entire body and mind are relaxing. I am going deeper and deeper into a state of deep relaxation. Every muscle in my body is now relaxing. Everything is peaceful and quiet.

One, the muscles of my face are relaxing.

Pause. (For 5 seconds)

Two, the muscles of my neck are slowly loosening and are relaxing.

Pause. (For 5 seconds)

Three, the muscles of my shoulders are losing their stiffness and are relaxing.

Pause. (For 5 seconds)

Four, the muscles of my hands are completely free and are relaxing.

Pause. (For 5 seconds)

Five, the muscles of my chest are relaxing.

Pause. (For 5 seconds)

Six, the muscles of my back and lower back are loosening and are relaxing.

Pause. (For 5 seconds)

Seven, the tension in my stomach is relaxing.

Pause. (For 5 seconds)

Eight, the muscles of my glutes are relaxing.

Pause. (For 5 seconds)

Nine, the muscles of my thighs are relaxing.

Pause. (For 5 seconds)

Ten, the muscles of my lower legs are relaxing.

Pause. (For 5 seconds)

[Repeat the following, three times]

I am now in a state of deep relaxation. I am falling deeper and deeper and deeper. From the top of my head to my legs, from my legs to my toes, from my toes to the bottom of my feet. My body is totally relaxed. Drifting deeper and deeper, I feel lighter and lighter, my mind is now quiet.

[Now is the time to create as many affirmation as you'd wish/need. Since you are trying to communicate with spirits a few of your affirmations could go like this...]

I am psychic.

I am loved and protected.

I trust my intuition.

I am a medium.

I have endless confidence in my psychic abilities.

[Repeat each affirmation ten or more times.]

[There is no need to record this part. Just keep calm and remain quiet. Use this time to let your imagination run wild. If you have the urge to think about your ancestors. Imagine them performing a task you've always remembered them doing, or imagine yourself walking through a door into another realm where you will meet your ancestor. Allow this visualization to go wherever it may.]

[Finish your recording with the statements written below.]

I will now come out of this state on the count of three, feeling refreshed and relaxed.

One, I am coming out of this state totally refreshed.

Two, I am now opening my eyes, fully energized.

Three, I am now in my normal conscious state, closer to my goals.

End of Self-Guided Meditation Script

Once you get used to this meditation and want to take it a step further you can then leave out the part about the affirmations and just allow yourself to drift deeper and deeper into the ethers of your imagination. The next form of communication that ancestors use to make contact is through dreams.

Dreams

The dream-realm goes by many names; the underworld, the subconscious/unconscious, wonderland, etc. Dreams are the most common and effective form of spiritual communication. During sleep your conscious mind is put to rest, silencing your inner critic responsible for linear thinking. Dreams are beyond the restrictions of this physical realm where the soul can express itself and the imagination is free. The dream-space is the playground where spirits and ancestors can communicate. Nothing is off limits, they are free to hang out with us in exciting locations, talk to us about any and everything and even show us what things are possible after the death of the physical body.

Dreams are doorways to the soul. There are many versions of what a soul may be but all explanations of the soul come to one agreement; that the soul is intangible. It is nearly impossible to describe. In describing what a soul is you limit its power thus destroying its context. The very idea of what a soul may be is what it symbolizes. Souls are the batteries responsible for life after death so much so to the point where they allow one to exist outside the known universe and all dimensions. Like raindrops that have merged with the vast waters of the ocean. The souls of your ancestors as well as your own are completely connected. Dreaming allows you to travel to the inner worlds of your psyche. You experience those worlds and their inhabitants without any limits. Dreams display images that represent both "realities" whether it is the outer (physical) or inner (non-physical/spiritual).

When you dream, countless images and symbols are expressed to illustrate a message. Your world is built and based upon what you believe, imagine and dream. Our understanding of dreams is only a drop in the bucket of infinite mystery. The soul, afterlife and dreams are all representations of what the imagination truly is – limitless. Before I explain how to contact your ancestors through dreams, it is important for you to understand that dreams operate on three levels of intensity. Understanding the levels of a dream can be used as a frame of reference when decoding your dreams.

The three levels are:

1st Level: The symbols and messages displayed in these types of dreams usually deal with day to day events. Your worldly issues are often revealed in these types of dreams such stress from work or relationships, moments of embarrassment, frustrating encounters with family members, etc. You can take these types of dreams literally and sometimes they reveal hidden emotional and mental aspects of self. For example, in your dream, you may remember being at the checkout in the grocery store and as you reach into your pocket to pay the cashier, your change goes flying everywhere. At first glance you may just scoff at the dreams as being non-sense, reminding you of some mundane event from earlier this month. If you look closer you may notice that this dream could be trying to tell you to look at the "change" around you. Or the dream could just be highlighting the same mundane events that happen in your waking life.

2nd Level: Dreams that occur at this level express symbols that are personal to the dreamer. Deep seated personal issues and long forgotten personal memories are expressed in this level. The exact memory of an incident may not occur in these types of dreams but the messages and symbols shown in the dream may express an old buried memory. These types of dreams have a bunch of randomness going on in them. Things may be out of place such as the people in the dream, the role you play in the dream, the activities you are doing in the dream, etc. In this layer of the dream most of the time you become aware that you're dreaming and may even control or predict what is going to occur in the dream. At this level of dreams, the symbols are personal to the dreamer, the use of a dream dictionary can only offer little assistance. These dreams require more introspection and meditation. Use your dream dictionary to gain further meaning behind a certain symbol but don't take any explanation that is outside of yourself as fact regarding these types of dreams. Go based on your feelings and study of self.

3rd Level: These dreams offer profound spiritual information. The themes and symbols illustrated in these types of dreams reside in the realm of the collective unconscious. The collective unconscious is the store house for all universal themes, ideas and symbols. World mythologies are housed here. They include stories, themes and symbols that correspond and relate to everyone and everything. A story from thousands of years ago about love and betrayal continues to resonate with people of today. Dream dictionaries and books about symbols are an excellent resource when searching for the message behind these dreams. The type of dreams that I've personally experienced at this level resonates with my spiritual path.

Dreams of deities, initiation, spirits and ancestors seem to come from this level. For example, I had a dream that I was in a temple located in a village in Africa. In the temple, this priest told me to go get water from the jungle and gave me a cup. Soon I was in the jungle and found a river. The cup was a golden color and I returned to the temple with the cup filled with water. Handing the cup of water to the priest, he then began pouring the water over my head and chanting something. He told me I'm a member of Jeru. Anyhow, when I exited the temple, the village seemed to be getting more intense with people planning on how they are going to escape because it seemed like a war was going to happen. When I awoke, I began to research things that could correspond with my dream. I came across various deities and one caught my eye, Mama Chola. A goddess of beauty, love and fertility. Colors associated with her are yellow, orange and amber. What stood out about my dream and this information is the gold cup I used in the dream to gather the water, that was used to "initiate" me. Suddenly, I remembered that I'd been studying the Kabbalah and Qlippoth and the name Jeru jumped out. I took this as short for Jerusalem which prompted me to look at the diagram of the tree of life. The middle sphere, Tiphareth, is beauty, harmony and compassion. These are traits I immediately associated with Mama Chola. Looking at this new information, I took it as the dream telling me that I was moving into a new sphere of consciousness, Tiphareth, and initiation out of the mysteries of Mama Chola which is represented by the sphere Netzach on the Kabbalah and A'arab Zaraq on the Qlippoth; which also represents the planet venus and Mama Chola along with other deities such as Erzulie and Oshun who are various forms of Venus.

Remember, only you can dictate what information pops out to you in your own dream that will lead you to your own revelations. Another confirmation for me about this dream is again the word Jerusalem. Jerusalem is referred to as the heart chakra of the world. Tiphareth, corresponds with the heart chakra; and the heart chakra operates as both an energy center and realm of Christ consciousness. Tiphareth is also the home of your holy guardian angel and a few weeks prior to the dream I performed a ritual known as The Bornless Ritual which helps one to merge with their holy guardian angel. This dream was just communicating with me based on all I was studying. Ultimately, I included this story of one of my dreams to illustrate to you how intricate the 3rd level of dreams can be; Just remain open and receptive. Below are exercises that will help you recall and decode your dreams;

How to Remember Your Dreams

Before going to sleep, create and repeat an affirmation. You can say internal or aloud, "I remember my dreams." Recording affirmations that are aimed at helping you remember your dreams is a great idea too. Another good technique to help remember your dreams is to treat your bedtime like a ritual. Begin going to sleep at the same time every night with the intention of remembering your dreams. Make it fun! Take a lovely bubble bath and listen to some soothing music before bed. Using essential oils and incenses will help you to relax before bed. Try drinking some Mugwort tea which helps to produce vivid dreams. If you're into tarot cards you can use your cards to decipher your dreams.

Easy & Quick Dream Tarot Spread

Grab your deck of tarot cards and begin to shuffle them. As you shuffle your cards state your intention for using your cards. You can state your intention either internally or aloud. Continue to shuffle the cards while concentrating on your intention. You can set your intention to simply wanting to know the meaning behind your dream. Stop shuffling when you deem it necessary to stop. Divide your cards into three separate stacks. Place each stack below the next. Take each stack and spread all the cards out into three rows. Look over each stack until you find your tarot deck's "Moon" card. The moon card is indicated by the number 18 (XVIII). Once you find the moon card take the card before the moon card and after it. Once you have all three cards, remove them from the deck and place them in order of 1-2-3. The card before the moon card is placed in the number 1 position, followed by the moon card in the number 2 position the card after the moon card in the number 3 position. The "moon" card in the second position doesn't have much meaning when decoding your dreams. Think of it as the compass that points you toward the cards that will tell you more about your dream. The first card represents "You" and your role in the dream you just had. The third card in this spread represents what the dream is trying to tell you. Use your intuition to help bring clarity to your reading. Try not to use text book definitions from tarot books to come to an understanding of what you're dreams meant. Dreams are abstract and most of the time shouldn't be taken literally. Using your intuition allowing you to receive impressions from the cards you've drawn. Go based on what feels right to you. Use tarot books, dream books and your intuition to guide you.

Soon you will notice that you will remember bits and pieces of your dreams. To keep the momentum going you can try to create something "concrete" to honor your dreams. Create an action that will allow you to remember the dream. If you're into music you can make a song about your dream or you can find a song and connect with the lyrics of the song that resonate with the message or feeling of the dream. If you enjoy writing, create a short story or piece of poetry about the dream. Dancing is a fun way of expression, you could act out the dream through your movements. Try any one of these or all three, there are no limits.

There are numerous exercises that can help you in remembering your dreams. Try the ones listed above or feel free to create your own. After all you know what is best for you!

How to Contact Your Ancestors in the Dream World

This exercise will take your dream adventures to the next level. You will now make a conscious effort to contact your ancestors via your dreams. To begin, you must first set an intention. The intention being to visit them. The writer Robert Moss gives many great methods and examples on how to communicate with the dearly departed through dreams. One of my favorite methods from his books is called, "The Dream Re-Entry Technique." Moss states that you must think of a dream as a "place". Somewhere you can traverse and experience. Next, you must build up your emotions by remembering something pleasant about the ancestor you wish to contact. If you're trying to contact your grandmother, try and remember something pleasant. You may remember one time when the both of you were outside enjoying a glass of freshly made iced tea. Remember how great you felt, the weather was warm, your grandmother shared funny stories from her past; the overall experience was loving and serene. Now use the emotions from that experience with your grandmother and channel it into having a dream. Ask to go on an adventure with her through the many dimensions of the dream world. You can come up with whatever you wish. Remain open to experiencing whatever may come to you. Know that you are protected and loved. Your ancestors and spirit guides are here to protect you, always and forever. Try this exercise every night until you get results. It may take a day, a week, a month or whenever – just know that you will breach the veil and contact your beloved ancestor. Robert Moss has a saying that is wonderful when thinking of our ancestors, he states, *"Our departed are living in the dreamworld, and they are dreaming of us."*

These exercises will give you quick results. Just set your intention, stating it as you lay in bed before sleep. State the name of the ancestor you want to talk to before going to sleep. Create a mantra to get your mind into a meditative state. Next create an emotion that corresponds with a positive experience with the ancestor you wish to contact – it can be a memory or something you wish you could've done while they were here or that you wish to do in the dreamworld. You'll be surprised at your results.

Assisting "Stuck" Ancestors

Hopefully, none of your ancestors will be stuck on this earthly realm after their death. I recommend working with ancestors that have obtained some form of spiritual knowledge of the universe and their place within it, to create your ancestral deity system. Those ancestors who are being honored and have gained spiritual knowledge via earth or the spiritual realms should be used to help those ancestors who are stuck in between worlds. Ancestors who already have spiritual awareness, who knows how to navigate the spirit world, have the information to reach and assist those ancestors who are stuck.

There are many ways someone can become "stuck" after death; lack of knowledge of the afterlife, an abrupt death, simply not accepting one's death, family's lack of ability to move on after the death of ancestor and so on. It is extremely important to heal any ill emotions you have towards the beloved ancestor you wish to contact. Emotions of deep sadness, grief and fear surrounding the death of a loved one aids the energy that keeps them trapped/stuck. Step 0 is very important; Meditation and working on balancing and cleansing your chakras will also help clear a lot of emotional and mental debris. You set the example and standard. You are the leader, if you aren't at your greatest or at least striving to be at your best, how can your ancestors be at their best and assist you? If one of your beloved ancestors is stuck in the ethers of the spirit world, follow the exercise below.

Your imagination will help loved ones who have passed over to the other side. Liberating the imagination of our beloved dead is the best method to help elevate them on the other side. Having no belief in life after death or remaining stuck in a controlled way of thinking such as believing in organized religion's idea of the afterlife is a sure way to get stuck on the other side. If your ancestor has a small or limited imagination it causes them to be separated from other vast spiritual realms. There are countless dimensions and worlds beyond the physical where one can reside after death. The imagination is the key to unlocking the gate to countless worlds/realities. A great imagination technique you can do to help your ancestors come to terms with death is to imagine them in your idea of the best heaven for them. For example, your favorite aunt you wish to work with and contact on the other side, loved to bake. A basic heaven for her would be one where she can bake the best desserts and taste exotic sweets. You can design any and everything in this realm. Visualize and imagine any and everything you can. Relish in her interactions and the emotions she feels. There are no limits to what you can do or create. You are vibrating from a place of love when connecting with your ancestors, the feeling of love, is too great to ignore – no matter where your ancestors reside in the afterlife they will feel the love you're radiating for them.

To help save an ancestor from residing in a realm that is based on established belief systems such as Christianity, Islam and others – you must first set the intention to travel and witness the realm in which they find themselves trapped or stuck in. You may be surprised by what you find. Some people are seen sitting in churches. Others may be experiencing something more extreme that relates to the religion that they've chose to associate with. You may find an ancestor in a realm that is reminiscent of the traditional version of Hell. To aid these ancestors, gather your spirit allies including other ancestors who are adept in navigating the afterlife. Calling on deities such as Hecate, Morpheus, Anubis or any spirit that deals with the death or the underworld can assist your quest to rescuing an ancestor. Just know that you are protected, loved and cannot fail.

Sometimes you will encounter ancestors who do not wish to move on from the realm they have created for themselves, no matter how limiting it may be. If an ancestor is afraid to move on they can create and reside in a dimension like the physical world they just left. But, in this world they may be participating in repetitious behavior that brings them comfort. From my own experience with my grandmother and trying to connect with her. I've had plenty of dreams where I'm at her home and its dimly lit kind of like an overcast and the feelings of gloom and boredom just seems to be everywhere in her house. She will often be seen sitting on the sofa or chair not really doing anything and not really wanting to do anything. The way she remained in this realm was the way she spent her last days on Earth. Just sitting around doing nothing. I've reached out to other ancestors who have transcended and know how to navigate the spiritual world and they've failed in getting her to move on.

My friend Sean told me a story about his uncle and how he refused to move on after his death. His uncle remained angry at his still living mother (Sean's grandmother) for not being the mother he wanted her to be and not giving him the funeral he wanted. Sean would have meetings with his uncle showing him ancient history and mythology that illustrates the power of melanated people in hopes to change the way he sees himself and help him move on from his attachment to his previous life. He even tried giving the grandmother a message from his uncle to try to calm the storm between them but his grandmother didn't care. Eventually, Sean gave up trying to help his uncle since he was just too stubborn to heed his advice and moved on. This is the true face of purgatory that is mentioned in religious texts. In the words of Dion Fortune, *"Purgatory is not a place, but a state of consciousness."*

You can only do so much to help someone transition before you must move on. Just because your ancestors no longer reside on Earth with a physical body doesn't make them smarter or more spiritual. Don't waste your time trying to help anyone who doesn't want to help themselves.

The final technique included in this book that will assist you in contacting your ancestors can be found in the back of this guide. It is titled, Robert Moss' Dream Re-Entry Technique. This exercise can be repeated every night before bed and will surely help you dream about your ancestors. It's the technique I used to contact my brother that I explained in detail in the section titled, Family Reunion.

All the techniques I've mentioned can be used and will help you contact your ancestors. Have fun and trust your intuition. You can create your own exercises and meditation and even modify the ones mentioned in this section. The choice is all yours.

STEP 5: RECOGNIZING DIVINITY

Recognizing the divinity of your beloved ancestors is the next step toward completing your system. At this point you should already have a few ancestors you wish to work with; which are the ancestors you've placed on your altar giving energy to. Now is the time to connect their endearing traits to attributes usually reserved for deities. This will allow you to identify your ancestors' power and get an idea of how they express their power and utilize such power.

Review which of your ancestors correlate with existing deities just to help give you more to identify with when filling in the information below. Think about some endearing traits about your beloved grandmother. If she was nurturing and kind she'd fit in the category of "great mother" deities. Maybe you have a special memory of her being there for you when you were sick. Add that memory to the trait of healing. Now you have a great mother energy with the power of healing.

The methods of contact given above will help you contact your ancestors to get the information needed below. Before you contact them maybe you can fill in some information based on memories of them. Think back on something that stood out about your ancestors. Did one enjoy gardening? Did one having healing hands and words? If you remember favorite plants, below list the name and attributes of the plants. If you know one was healing, healing is associated with water which an element you can use to correspond with the abilities of the appropriate ancestor. Look at the memories of your ancestors to find traits that can help you comprehend the power they possess in the afterlife. Favorite animals, colors and such can be placed in its corresponding section.

Fill in as much information as you can below for all the ancestors you are using to build your ancestral system. Once you've completed a list on your own it is now time to move on to contacting your ancestors directly so that you can continue to empower them, helping them develop in the spirit world which also helps you grow in both the physical and spiritual world. The information you will gather below will help to make your spiritual power and that of your ancestors – tangible.

Creating Your Ancestral System

Primal Name: can be referred to as the soul name of your ancestor. It's a very sacred name that is believed to be the true name of our soul before any lifetime and incarnation. Your ancestors who have acquired enough knowledge of their true origins and their place in the universe will have access to their primal/soul name. The words of the names you will receive may shock you because they mostly don't correlate with the human language or any other earthly language. If you don't receive the primal name from an ancestor then they should study themselves and the universe more. Once you acquire this bit of information it's best to keep it to yourself unless stated by your ancestors that it is okay to share it with others.

Origin: do not confuse this part of the system with a physical origin but think of it as a marker to help you identify certain attributes of your own ancestors. This section will help you connect the dots on many things dealing with your ancestors' powers. When discussing the details of my brother, I mentioned voodoo, The Maroon people and Chinese symbols. He told me his soul/primal name which has a relation to a physical Asian country but if I literally interpret the country associated with is name and use that as a foundation for all the information I could gather to illustrate to his power then I wouldn't get too far. By giving you a physical country/continent your ancestors give you more tools to use to comprehend their power through symbols associated with the culture, mythology and history of the given landmass. An ancestor may tell that their origin is in ancient China. Look at this to establish a connection with their power. Research all that interest you about ancient China; myths and symbols of ancient China and see if any of those symbols may have been relevant in the life of the ancestor that gave you this information. After researching ancient Chinese myths, you may come across Kwan

Yin the goddess of Compassion. You may remember the compassion an ancestor bestowed not only to you but all those they encountered. The more you research about Kwan Yin, you may find that the peacock is associated with this goddess. The peacock is a bird that may connect with your ancestor and upon researching the symbolism around the peacock you are given more insight into the depth of that ancestor's power. Any symbols that resonate with you that identifies with the power of your ancestors should be placed on your ancestor altar.

Colors: the color(s) they enjoyed as they lived on earth can be the color that represents and empowers them in the spirit world. Each color has various traits that can be used to describe the many attributes of your ancestors. Burgundy may be a color given to you by an ancestor as a favorite or preferred color. Burgundy is a color that represents fierce power, explosive energy and strength. It's also a color associated with warriors. You can analyze traits of an ancestor to bring more clarity behind the colors that represent them as a spiritual entity. If you have an origin to associate with your ancestor you may be able to gain more understanding of the color burgundy within that country or culture given in the origin section. The warrior energy of burgundy could lead you to look at warriors in the country/culture given in the origin section and give you more traits to associate with the power of your ancestor. Don't stop at what you find while researching in these books – ask your ancestors for answers.

Emblems: are images/symbols used to define the energy of your ancestors. Again, this helps to bring more clarity to your mind about the power of your ancestors which is ultimately within yourself. But, to utilize that power a symbol must be associated with it to understand it. When you're given an image or symbol of something it helps to build a better understanding around it because there are traits that are associated with the image that adds definition. Your cousin may have loved water, had many pictures of fish, loved to fish and told you through channeling that she is represented by a fish. Deities associated with fish are; the great mother goddess known as Yemaya, the Goddess of the Ocean and a great mother figure. Nu, the Egyptian great mother also known as the goddess of the abyss just to name a few. Look at these deities as a representation of your power and your ancestors' power but by no means are you nor your ancestors limited to only the characteristics given to these deities. This information is only used to give you further understanding of your power and the power of your ancestors. My brother's energy is associated with a dragon which I associated with the Khmer Neak dragon.

Plants: this includes trees, flowers and herbs. It is just another symbol/item you can place on your ancestor altar to help resonate with the power of various ancestors. Each ancestor may have a certain plant that they may have enjoyed while on earth as well as one that gives further insight into their spiritual power. Maybe your grandmother loved Lavender, using it to calm her in stressful situations. Try placing a lavender plant or oil on your ancestor altar to help soothe your grandmother and ancestors as they continue their journey in the afterlife. The lavender placed on your altar can become infused with the power of your ancestors and used for rituals and other things.

Minerals: crystals or gemstones of any kind. Again, the origin you were given may hold a deeper meaning behind the crystals/gemstones you were given by your ancestors. Any crystals you are given by your ancestor can be used in your ancestor pot. In Step 6, further details are explained on how to build your ancestor pot. Any crystals/gemstones that are used to identify with the power of your ancestors helps to raise your vibrations which increases your spiritual protection and other benefits.

Element: the four elements are fire, earth, water and air. An ancestor can identify with any element. With each ancestor, assign an element that corresponds with the physical birth month of an ancestor if you are unclear on which element to identify with your ancestor. Once you get into the habit of communicating with your ancestors regularly you will receive which element you can use to identify their power.

Fire governs primal energy, spirituality and creativity.

Water governs emotions, feelings and consciousness.

Air governs the mind (mental), power and action.

Earth governs nature and the material/physical world.

Offerings: any food that your ancestors enjoyed during their time on earth is the food you should be offering to them. Ask your ancestors what food they would like. Candy is another treat that can be used to empower your ancestors. Candy symbolizes luck, pleasure, happiness and sweetness. Spirits such as rum, vodka, wine and beer are great items to offer to your ancestors. According to Terrence McKenna from his book, Food of the Gods, in the section about wine, he states; *"its powers of exhilaration and intoxication were thought to be manifestations of divine possession."* Pouring or spiting libations to your ancestors is a great way to invoke and empower them.

Uses/Fuction: prosperity, protection, healing, knowledge, etc. Ask each ancestor you choose to work with – what they can help you with. If you grandmother was compassionate and had a knack for healing anyone who was sick; perhaps her power in the afterlife would be one of healing and compassion. If that is the case you wouldn't use her to assist you in a hex or curse. Everyone has their purpose; each ancestor has their own abilities in which they function at their best. We all have certain things we are good at. I'm not too good at math so you wouldn't put me in charge of accounting. The same goes for spirits/ancestors that have their functions. Just look at the people in your life right now. You know who you can call about certain things and who not to call. The same applies here.

The deities given in mythology and spiritual systems represent power that already resides within you and your ancestors. I'm sure even at this very moment you have a deity who you identify with more than another. One that you feel connected to more than others. I'm my case I've always been intrigued with the goddess Persephone. But this doesn't exclude me from invoking and utilizing the power of other deities. Deities, spirits, demons, angels, etc. are all created to catalog your own abilities. They are nothing more than the same energy you have access to that has been classified so that you can comprehend your own power. How could you know how great you are if you couldn't explain, describe or comprehend your own divinity? Your ancestors are another expression of that same divine power.

STEP 6: APPLYING YOUR SYSTEM

Creating your own rituals is a great way to empower your ancestors. Remember, that the intention behind your rituals should be to 'feed" your ancestors. Creating your ancestor altar is a ritual. Pouring libations and serving food to them is a ritual. Many people perform a ritual to a well-known deity to manifest something, usually in the form of money, a job or relationship. Doing this with limited imagination, believing that the entity/deity they are performing these rituals for is external and beyond their realm of control.

You're crafting rituals for your ancestors to invoke and empower them which empowers you. The rituals you create are channels that will broaden your awareness of your ancestors and their power. They don't need to be fed a ritual to complete a task. They don't feed off your energy that way. Feeding your ancestors with rituals allows you to become more aware of their energy, empowering you thus giving you more power to attract what you need and want in your life.

What is A Ritual?

The dictionary definition of a ritual is *"a religious or solemn ceremony consisting of a series of actions performed according to a prescribed order."* Another definition of a ritual is *"an act or series of acts regularly repeated in a set precise manner."* Based on this definition a ritual can consist of anything done in a repeated manner. Plays and movies are rituals performed by actors to produce a result, which is to invoke certain emotions and actions from the audience. Sporting events and award shows such as the Superbowl, NBA Finals, Grammy's and The Oscars are rituals that invoke strong feelings from all that engage in the fanfare. Brushing your teeth every morning or eating dinner at the same time every night is a ritual. Donald Tyson in his book titled, Ritual Magic, he states that a ritual is *"the medium through which the art of magic is practiced. It consists of an action or series of actions, which may be entirely mental or mental and physical, whereby the power of magic is released and directed towards the fulfillment of a specific desire."* By conducting a ritual, you are just applying your intent, directing your thoughts and through controlled action to produce a desirable result. Author D.J. Conway in her book, The Ancient and Shining Ones, she states that a ritual is *"merely the taking of energy from another plane of existence and weaving that energy, by specific thoughts, words and practices, into a desired physical form or result in this plane of existence. The whole idea of magick is to contact various energy pools* (Gods/Goddesses) *that exist in a dimension* (subconscious mind) *other than your own."*

Your purpose for conducting a ritual is to produce change. It is advised that you create your own rituals since the power of your ancestors is unique to your spiritual pursuits and knowledge as well as the spiritual maturity and attainment of the ancestors you wish to use for ritual work. To create your own ritual the use of symbols is a must. Whatever you choose to use during your ritual corresponds with the energy of the vast spiritual worlds. When you create and perform a ritual you are harnessing the power of your subconscious mind which is the creative store house that allows magick to manifest. The subconscious mind comprehends and communicates in symbols. The symbols you choose to use in your ritual must represent something that corresponds with the specific ancestral energy. Colors, incense, images, plants, food/drink and other tools aid the subconscious mind in communicating with the specific energy you want to channel. Use the information you've gathered in Step 5 as your foundation for your rituals.

Creativity and emotions are very important for your rituals. With your creativity, you breathe life into your ritual by drawing meaning from the various symbols you find meaning in to use for your rituals. The more controlled your emotions are for the ritual the more effective your results will be. By controlled, this doesn't mean emotionally stale or dull. You must be emotionally stable, sound and energetic. That's why is it important that you've done appropriate self-development (balancing chakras, ridding trauma and ill-thoughts and feelings) before you begin to contact spirits. If you don't know how you feel or can't control your thoughts or emotions, how in the hell are you going to effectively stimulate and comprehend the energy you wish to connect with? Confidence, self-confidence in yourself and your abilities will help you become better at communicating with spirits and your ancestors. You'll be communicating with energies that know you and love you. Feel comfortable enough to talk to them in the manner you would talk to a loved one or best friend, which should boost your confidence in performing your rituals. No need for dramatic formalities, your confidence should come from a place of feeling equal to your ancestors. Remember, this isn't ancestor worship in the classical sense of worshipping those who've come before you in a religious sense. Nor is it to discredit you as a powerful entity with his or her own primal power. When communicating with your ancestors you are their equal. They once had a physical body and know the ills of this world/humanity, you are still bound to a physical body and must continue to endure the ills of humanity until it is your time to make the transition. No melaninated person is greater or lesser than the other. I dare say that the only ones who can be viewed as "less" are the ones who wish to glorify their human experience as if it holds any real importance over their own divinity.

You are not defined by the multiple lifetimes you've endured or your limited perception of yourself and your cosmic birthright. You are not who you've been programmed to believe you are; your ancestors are not the people you previously believe them to be. Your ancestors including yourself; are greater than you've ever imagined. There is no separation between you and the cosmic energy of the universe and beyond. Creating your own ancestral deity system allows you to develop this mindset. Let's get into creating some rituals for your beloved ancestors.

Ancestor Pot

An ancestor pot is called many things such as; spirit pot, soul pot and ancestor spirit bottle. Whatever name you wish to use, it still serves the same purpose of contacting and connecting you to the world of the ancestors. Your ancestor pot will act as a bridge to your ancestors, used to ground and manifest their energy allowing their work and help to manifest swiftly and easily. Your ancestors will help you with many things in your life. The ancestor pot you will craft and place on your altar will help bring their blessings straight to you. You will be able to use this pot for any type of spell you wish to conduct whether it is for money, love, hexes or anything else you can imagine.

A quick spell you can do is place the picture of someone who continues to bother you into your ancestor pot and begin expressing your problems with that individual – soon you will see that the person who was bothering you is no longer a threat. Want to increase the attraction power you have over someone, add an item you wish to give the person of your affection to your ancestor pot with the intention of making this person yours. Once you completed your ritual, give the item you've placed in your ancestor pot to your admirer and watch their feelings for you increase. You can do whatever your imagination leads you to do with your ancestor pot. The only limits you'll have with your ancestor pot are the ones you create. Your ancestors are always here to help whenever you need them to. The supplies needed for creating your own ancestor pot are:

A vessel, something you can use to hold items in such as a glass/ceramic jar or pot (with a lid). A small to medium sized cauldron with a lid will work too. I like black jars or pots so the contents of the pot aren't visible.

Herbs that are connected to the afterlife, death and communicating with spirits. A few herbs you can add to your ancestor pot include – Basil (for love, courage and protection), Mugwort (helps with clairvoyance), Myrrh (used in ancient embalming techniques), Wormwood (healing, removes fear of death) and Valerian root (which is associated with sleep and can be used as a substitute for actual graveyard dirt). There are plenty of herbs that you can add to your ancestor pot. A book on magical herbs will give you more of an idea on what other herbs you can add.

Gemstones or crystals such as clear quartz, amethyst or rose quartz just to name a few. Crystals/gemstones will help in creating a positive environment so that you can receive the high vibration messages from your dearly departed. They also clear the air of negativity. You can even add a crystal in the shape of a skull to represent the physical remains of your ancestors. Any of the minerals given to you by your ancestors in Step 5 will help to concentrate your ancestral energy into your pot.

Dirt from the grave of your ancestors. You can get the dirt from various physical graves of some of your favorite ancestors. You can even just grab the dirt from the grave of the head of your family such as a grandmother or grandfather – since our grandparents serve as the main vein of the modern family tree. If you do not wish to go to the graveyard to retrieve the dirt of an ancestor you can make your own graveyard dirt. This recipe for graveyard dirt is unconventional. To create your own graveyard dirt, you will need fresh soil perhaps from your garden or anywhere. Once you've gotten your dirt, add it to a vessel, grab a piece of paper and rip it into various strips. Write the names of each ancestors you are working with on each piece of paper. Add the strips into the dirt and light a candle. A white candle will do since it represents death in ancient cultures but also purity and peace.

Begin to meditate, chant or pray over the dirt. Mourning and remembering your beloved deceased. Hold your own funeral and eulogy for your dearly departed. You can continue to do this for as long as you wish. 3 days is enough time to mourn your dearly departed. Once the mourning has concluded your graveyard dirt is now ready.

Take all the ingredients and add them to your ancestor pot. It is good to do this step adding each ingredient one by one. Before you begin adding your items remember to purify the vessel. Spray the vessel you're using as your ancestor pot with Florida water helping to remove any stagnant energy. You can use any item that is used to rid negative energy to cleanse your ancestor pot. Once your vessel is clean, add your graveyard dirt. Mix into the graveyard dirt the various herbs you have that correspond with the overall intent of your ancestor pot. All the herbs dealing with death, ancestors, the afterlife, funerals and spirits should be added and mixed into your graveyard dirt. Use a spoon, stick or whatever to mix the herbs and dirt together in the vessel. All the while mixing just visualize all the energy of each item intermingling with one another. Next, you can arrange the gemstones that correspond with your ancestors in any order into your pot. You can arrange them all in a circle in the pot with a quartz gemstone skull in the center. This represents the remains of your ancestors. That's all it takes. You can add music while you make your ancestor pot, light candles and incense to put you into a magical mood. To feed/empower your ancestor pot, you could pour a bit of liquor into the pot. Rum, whiskey or whatever spirit you like can be used. Meditating and talking to your ancestor pot will empower it. It acts as a beacon to your ancestors and can be used to represent them while you communicate your problems to it and gather ideas and inspiration on how to solve your problems and increases your quality of life.

Ancestor Fun Night

This is an awesome ritual that will help you become accustomed to feeling the energy of your ancestors on a day to day basis. To begin you must pick a day of the week that will be your designated "Ancestor Fun Night." It can be any day of the week just make sure you can use this day every week to spend uninterrupted time with your ancestors. Let's say you've chosen Wednesday as your weekly "ancestor fun night" because it is the day of your weekly favorite TV show that comes on and you think a few of your ancestors may enjoy watching this show with you. You can create and enjoy games and other fun task such as cooking, dancing, writing or whatever you wish. This can be a day where you watch certain movies that a few of your ancestors may have enjoyed. You could drink their favorite liquor on this day, cook their favorite meal and serve it to your ancestors as a gesture of love and honor.

While participating in various activities you can talk to your ancestors as if they are physically in the room with you. Although you no longer can see them with your physical eyes they are still with you. The more time you spend with your ancestors and continue to conduct and participate in your weekly "Ancestor Fun Night" you will begin to feel their energy around you. As you continue to open yourself up to the energy of your ancestors you will soon experience their energy all the time. It may feel like it is radiating around you, some may experience a feeling from deep inside them as a warm and fuzzy feeling radiating from the heart center. This is the feeling of eternal love. Your ancestors reside in a realm of immeasurable love. Allow yourself to celebrate this feeling.

Active Imagination

Robert A. Johnson has a book titled, <u>Inner Work</u>, which goes into detail about how to explore your inner self through the power of your very own imagination. Practicing active imagination daily will change your life, it gives you the power to resolve your own personal issues using your own vivid imagination. You create your own story with your own characters. You give yourself the power to decode the meaning of symbols that give you all the answers to your intimate questions. The stories you craft are not fictional – they are messages expressed symbolically from the deep depths of your subconscious mind. Active Imagination is a healthy way of expressing parts of yourself that are unable to be explored in your daily physical life. You can use active imagination to help with any emotional/spiritual difficulties you may be facing. You can use the following instructions to help you with any issue but I'm going to discuss how active imagination can be used as a gateway to communicate with your ancestors.

Before you begin your adventure into the realms of your imagination to meet your ancestors, you must first decide a method you will use to record your journey. You can either use a voice/video recorder or write down your encounter as you experience it. Decide which method gives you the most comfort. You can even switch up the way you choose to record your active imagination sessions with voice recording for 1 to 2 days followed by a few days of writing out each session. Do whatever you want. Once you decide the best way to record your sessions; you must now create a relaxing setting. Think of your active imagination session as a personal ritual and with a ritual you must treat it with respect. Put yourself in a ritual mood, light some incense that will help stimulate your pineal gland like lotus or sandalwood. Light a few candles to add to the ambience. The best time of day to do this is when you will not be disturbed. Designate about an hour of free time to conduct your active imagination session. Change into comfortable clothes, add some music, perform a relaxing meditation to clear your mind and program your intention to release any thoughts that may interfere with your active imagination session. Once you feel relaxed, grab your pen and paper or if you're using a recording device then press play. Sit for a moment and explore your imagination – let your mind wander and take you wherever it may. Don't worry about writing a fantasy story that you wish to show off to someone, don't even worry about your spelling or grammar. Write it how you would write something only your eyes will see. After all you are writing for yourself, you will need to be able to understand what you wrote about yourself. Active imagination will help you to understand yourself more and uncover the meaning behind the symbols oozing from your subconscious.

Now you're ready to contact an ancestor through active imagination. To begin you must clear and calm your mind through a quick meditation. One of the best that will help accomplish a clear mind quickly is to count backwards from ten while imagining yourself walking down a flight of stairs. With each step, see the number pop into your mind counting back from ten. Continue all the way until you reach zero. Once you reach zero you can say, "I am now calm and centered." Now you're ready for the next step, to contact an ancestor. Now that you are centered and calm, grab your notebook or tape/video recorder and relax. Set the intention to contact a specific ancestor. You should establish contact with an ancestor you were close with during their time on earth. This is best due to the established emotional connection between you and this ancestor. The emotional cord you both share is a link. A link that will allow more fluid contact and better communication. The ancestor you shared a close connection with is just as excited to talk to you as you are them. Just as Robert Moss has stated in his books, *"The dead are dreaming of us."*

Once your intention has been made, allow your mind to wander. Think about the ancestor you are choosing to contact. Imagine the type of clothing they used to wear, imagine anything you want about them. As you imagine all these things allow your imagination to expand however it chooses to. You can imagine that the two of you are sitting in the backyard of your childhood home. As you imagine this, try to start a conversation. What do you say? What does your ancestor say? Write it all in your notebook or say it into your tape/video recorder.

Another method to contact an ancestor is to create a neutral space for your ancestor to meet you. Imagine you are somewhere calm and peaceful, better yet go to a place that gives you a sense of nostalgia. It could be a party at a relatives' house that you had good memories of. I like to imagine I'm in front of a doorway that has the name of the ancestor I wish to see on the door. I look at the door and imagine every little detail about the door. Placing my hand on the door knob, I feel the cold sensation of the brass door knob and the emotion of excitement I feel as I begin to turn the knob. As the door opens I allow my imagination to run wild and guide me.

Your imagination is your kingdom, you can build and do whatever you wish. Begin to record this awesome place in your journal or through your tape/video recorder. Write down every detail that is worth noting. You are not trying to write an essay or a novel. Relax and write in whichever way is comfortable for you. Your active imagination sessions are for your eyes only. You are recording these sessions so that you may decode them later and find out their spiritual meaning/messages to further guide you on your own spiritual journey. No need to be wordy and dramatic. Just write what you feel and what you're experiencing. As you describe your special place where you wish to meet your ancestor, allow your imagination to continue to unfold. Soon you may find that the ancestor you wish to talk is now with you. Continue to use your imagination and record what happens next. What do they say? Is there anything different about them? Be sure to write/record whatever you experience. If you're having a bit of trouble jumpstarting your imagination try this:

Remember something that you may have experienced with the ancestor you wish to contact. Relive that memory, replay it over in your mind. Just before the memory ends, change it by adding something different like a new conversation or objects. You can even try to change the entire memory into something else. This is a surefire way of jumpstarting your imagination. There is no right or wrong way of conducting or experiencing active imagination. If you are using a notebook or journal just write what you feel and experience during your active imagination adventure. If you are using a tape or video recorder just verbally explain in detail whatever is going on in your active imagination adventure. There is no right or wrong way to conduct an active imagination session. Just relax and allow your imagination to roam free. If that fails you can just fake it until you make it. Just act as if you are talking with your ancestor. You can be as detailed as you want. Control everything about your encounter through your imagination. The same energy you are using to act out this encounter with your ancestor still resides in the realm of your imagination. If you still have trouble with your imagination, check out the sample I've written below to jumpstart your imagination.

"The room is warm and cozy just as I remember. The scent of lavender fills my nose, it smells just like my grandmother's house. The kitchen chairs are still stiff. I turn around and see the same yellow wallpaper all around me. The sink is clean with no dishes in sight. It's light outside, the open window allows a cool breeze to enter. I wish to talk to my grandmother, to see her for the first time in years. I remember her beautiful brown hair, with spots of gray. She used to hate the gray but it reminded me of wisdom. She was very wise always giving the best advice. I look around the room and my eyes land on her favorite painting of a vase of roses. I don't remember this picture being in the kitchen. I walk closer to the picture to inspect it. This picture reminds me so much of my grandmother...oh how I miss her. Someone clears their throat, it sounds like it's behind me. I turn around and see her. My grandmother just the way I remember her. She is smiling, it's bright exactly how I remember it.

GRANDMOTHER: *It's so wonderful to see you. I've missed you so much. We have a lot to talk about.*

ME: *I've missed you so much more. You look good, I can't believe this is happening.*

I hug her and she returns the hug tightly as if to never let me go..."

This is only a sample to get you on the right track with your active imagination sessions. A great way to tell who is talking during your active imagination sessions is to write the name of the ancestor you are communicating with just as it is written above. You can even use abbreviations or the names of the ancestors you encounter. After you've ended your session it is your responsibility to go back and analyze what was written. You are the only person who can extract any meaning behind what was revealed in your session. Using the above example to further illustrate how to uncover and decode the symbolism within your active imagination session is to reread the session and look for anything that stands out to you that you may want to inspect; Looking at the above example let's look at the item, lavender. It is best to look at which items stand out to you and write out your own personal meaning of each. Lavender may be a scent that reminds you of your grandmother, it is calming, warm and welcoming. Which are all the traits that come to mind when thinking about your grandmother. Upon researching the spiritual meaning behind lavender, you may find that it helps with spiritual and emotional blockages along with raising vibrations and accessing higher consciousness. From here you can go on to investigate more about your session and the multiple meanings of the symbols given to you in your session and how they relate to you and what they're trying to tell you.

Accessing the realm of the ancestors allows you to become aware of your inner power. Active imagination and other methods given in this book will allow you to release your inner power.

Personal Mythology

"Each time you add your own science you give to your own plight."
–Brother Panic

Myths, fairy tales, folk tales, legends, lore... whatever you want to call it, all describe the same thing – the divine power that resonates within you. Think of them as stories based on dreams of an entire civilization. Many of the civilizations that these stories originated from may be gone but the spirit of these stories remain and continue to expand. Myths and fairy tales not only teach lessons or illustrate your divine power, they are pure symbolic expressions of your power. Even what is expressed in these stories is only the tip of the iceberg. Creating your own personal mythology involving your beloved ancestors allows for pre-existing myths to be improved and adapted.

To begin crafting your ancestors' personal mythology you must first analyze archetypes. Carl Jung described archetypes as *"a universal and recurring image, pattern or motif representing a typical human experience."* We all demonstrate traits from various archetypes. As we age we fall in and out of various archetypes, and as our lives and circumstances change, different phases in our lives require different types of energies. Our life is a story and we all are participating in our very own cosmic drama. There are tons of archetypes but for the sake of time and space, the most common archetypes will be highlighted.

- The Hero: is the main character of his or her own story. At the beginning of their journey they will be prompted to leave their familiar world and travel into new and uncharted lands. What the hero experiences in the new world will change them forever, usually the change helps them on their journey so they can complete their story. The hero's journey is full of sacrifice, they must grow, find love and/or purpose. High risk, high reward is the order of the day for the hero. Anti-Heroes count here as well. You may categorize them as rebels since they can be an outlaw or villain to society or a group of people. But anti-heroes often have the same goal in mind as a typical hero to save someone or themselves or to possibly overcome some inner turmoil. Anti-heroes often fail and their journey serves as a reminder of what to do and avoid whether it is situations or people.

- The Mentor: The wise companion of the hero. Often comes in the form of an old lady or man. The mentor is full of advice, constantly guiding the hero on his journey. You can see this individual as the inner voice of the hero. When the hero is lost or indecisive during his adventure, he will often remember the guidance of the mentor and draw inspiration from their wise words. There is room for multiple mentors including flawed mentors that show the hero what to avoid on his or her journey.

- The Messenger: provides challenges to the hero in the form of a message or event. The way in which the messenger pops up and what she must deliver adds personality to the hero and his story. The call to adventure is jump started by the messenger and this event prompts the hero to begin on his journey. Depending on how the hero responds to the call of the messenger, sets the stage for later conflict between the hero and himself. Messengers in stories can come in the form of people, events or information. The job of the messenger is to shift the story, to add more weight to the hero, testing his endurance. The messenger jumpstarts the story and motivates the hero.

- The Trickster/Shapeshifters: is the agent of change! She is full of tricks and "evil" deeds. Tricksters are very funny and help to purify the ego of the hero. The trickster mocks the "system" and works to destroy structure and rules. Usually the alliance of the trickster is cloudy – neither working exclusively for the hero or the villain (shadow). Her intentions remain questionable. She usually has a lesson to teach that is not always apparent at first glance. She can shapeshift such as changing appearances, behavior and mood. Ultimately adding drama to the story and journey of the hero. The trickster helps to bring about great change within the hero due to these antics. Shapeshifters are flexible, they can be anyone in the hero's story and offer a wide variety of encounters, advice and growth. Tricksters and shapeshifters represent repressed traits that is often expressed in powerful and mythic forms such as monsters, demons, god/desses; or in mundane forms - family members or lovers. Tricksters and shapeshifters are the raw expressions of your subconscious/unconscious mind. Providing change and transformation for the hero is the goal of the trickster/shapeshifter.

- Threshold Guardians: are commonly perceived as enemies of the hero. But they function as obstacles that the hero must overcome. Think of them as mini villains, those the hero fights on his journey to defeat the ultimate evil. They are also allies that the hero must recruit to help him on his journey. Whether the hero must fight them or complete some sort of task for them, they always bestow advice that is critical to the development of the hero. The hero grows stronger in his own power as well as collectively due to his newfound ally, teammate, sidekick. Threshold Guardians represent deep emotional wounds, self-limitations or inner demons that prevent you from progressing on your journey. They're here to test you to determine if you are truly ready to challenge yourself and change.

- The Shadow: the villain/threat of the story and to the hero. In traditional stories the shadow is represented as an external enemy but metaphorically the shadow represents repressed, rejected, unexpressed aspects of the hero. Just like the threshold guardians mentioned above, the shadow can represent deep emotional trauma and fear that has the potential to "destroy" the hero. The shadow acts as a conduit for the greatest change not only within the hero but the universe in which the hero's journey and the story is set. The intentions of the hero and the shadow often merge and the line between good and evil begin to blur. Often the hero can begin to look like the villain due to the intentions and reasons behind his journey while the villain would begin to look righteous and justified in his actions and quest. Monsters and demons can be expressed as shadow entities representing the dark part of the hero, the unexpressed potential that has been collected and stored until the day it must be exorcised by the light of consciousness.

This is the main group of archetypes. There are many more archetypes including: the lover, the magician, the rebel, the fairy godmother, etc. When aligning your ancestors with an archetype please note that you don't have to be rigid. If you believe your favorite uncle to be a wise mentor based on your memories of him and his personality during his earthly incarnation, doesn't mean he identifies with the wise mentor archetype in the afterlife. Look at the archetypes as placeholders of the various characters in the great cosmic story that is your life. One moment your uncle may be the wise mentor who gives advice to you on your spiritual path and once you learned what you needed to learn to go to another level, your beloved uncle who is your wise mentor may become the rebel aiding you in defeating your shadow. But, for now keep it simple. Just align the ancestors you wish to work with, with corresponding archetypes so you can build a foundation for your personal mythology. Once your foundation is laid out, you can change your story and characters accordingly. Look at the archetypes as various traits of the hero. These archetypes are hidden somewhere within the hero but it takes an archetype to appear to make the abilities (expressed by the archetype) to manifest within the hero and/or within the hero's life. Apply this same method of thinking to the powers that you and your ancestors possess.

You are the hero in your personal mythology while the ancestors can take the roles of the various archetypes that are scattered among the hero's journey. A wise mother, uncle, grandmother or whoever you wish can take the role of the mentor – you can have many mentors. Siblings, cousins and friends could take the role as trickster/shapeshifter. The shadow can be parts of yourself that your refuse to acknowledge or even past traumas that are still holding you back emotionally, mentally and spirituality. These issues can take the form of an abusive ancestor who wronged you during their time on earth and the issues are still not resolved. Working with the ancestor who has abused or wronged you as the archetypical shadow in your personal mythology will be the hero slaying the shadow. Once you've healed from that trauma, you've released a huge burden on yourself and that ancestor thus allowing you to channel any newfound energy given by that ancestor.

The next piece needed for creating your personal mythology is the hero's journey. The complete journey of the hero are stages that the hero must go on in his or her journey. This outline was identified by Joseph Campbell as the fundamentals for storytelling and myth. The stages of the hero's journey are:

1. **The Ordinary World**. Is where the background of the hero is shown, setting the stage for the hero and the tone for the story. Opposition is stirring in the hero's life causing stress and leading him down and perceived unstable path.
2. **The Call to Adventure**. The catalyst that gets the story moving. The messenger brings a message that sets off a series of events causing the hero to begin his journey.
3. **Refusal of the Call**. The hero feels the fear of the unknown and tries to turn away from the adventure. Alternately,

another character (minor archetype) may express the uncertainty and danger ahead.

4. **Meeting with the Mentor**. The hero comes across a seasoned traveler of the worlds who gives him or her training, equipment or advice that will help on the journey. Or the hero reaches within to a source of courage and wisdom.

5. **Crossing the Threshold**. The hero commits to leaving the Ordinary World and entering a new region or condition with unfamiliar rules and values.

6. **Tests, Allies and Enemies**. The hero is tested and sorts out allegiances with the special world.

7. **Approach**. The hero and newfound allies prepare for the major challenge in the special world.

8. **The Ordeal**. Near the middle of the story, the hero enters a central space in the Special World and confronts death or faces his or her greatest fear. Out of the moment of death comes a new life.

9. **The Reward.** The hero takes possession of the treasure won by facing death. There may be celebration, but there is also danger of losing the treasure again.

10. **The Road Back**. The hero is driven to complete the adventure, leaving the Special World to be sure the treasure is brought home.

11. **The Resurrection**. At the climax, the hero is severely tested once more on the threshold of home. He or she is purified by a last sacrifice, another moment of death and rebirth, but on a higher and more complete level. By the hero's action, the polarities that were in conflict at the beginning are finally resolved.

12. **Return with the Elixir**. The hero returns home or continue the journey, bearing some element of the treasure that has the power to transform the world as the hero has been transformed.

Archetypes and the stages of the hero's journey are key to creating an engaging mythological story. The steps given above are only guidelines to help you achieve your personal mythology for yourself and your ancestors. Researching the life of more famous ancestors such as Tupac Shakur or Jimi Hendrix will help to draw inspiration on how to craft the mythology of the ancestors you're working with personally. Let's look at Tupac Shakur.

You may not look at him in the classical sense as a hero; slaying the monster that threatens the world and living happily ever after with his eternal love. His mythology is remixed from the traditional stories. Tupac is a hero to all those he represents which are the oppressed people within society – most notably the indigenous people of the world aka black and brown folks. You can even line him up with mythological figures such as Shiva, Krishna and Jesus; since he gives hope to the down-trotted and speaks truth and carries the message of consciousness in his words and actions. Just as it is mentioned in Step 5 of this book, lining up your ancestors with a known deity helps for you to identify with the symbols that your ancestor is trying to communicate to you. If you connect the Hindu god Shiva with Tupac you will see many similarities. Shiva is the consort of the great mother goddess Kali – who is the goddess of creation and destruction. Although Shiva is Kali's consort he has other goddesses as his mate. Looking back on Tupac's life, he had many women around. Just like Kali, Shiva has a similar contrast of representing both creation and destruction – in Tupac's lyrics of various songs you can hear the differences between the messages he is trying to express to his listeners. One minute he's telling everyone to "keep their head up" and the next song he's rapping about "fuck the police and we don't love these hoes." His entire career is a huge contradiction. You can even expand that to his life. His upbringing of being the son from an acclaimed family deeply rooted within the black panther party and rising to be the god of Thug Life.

Historically, Kali is worshipped by a cult known as the Thuggees or Thugs where robbery and murder were considered their religious duty. The duration of their reign was from 1200 A.D. or before to about the 1800s; a couple hundred years later, we have Tupac gracing the world with hits like, "Brenda's Got a Baby" and "Hail Mary" all the while posing with a thug life tattoo on his abdomen and wearing a bandana, reminiscent of the head-wraps worn by the ancient Thuggees so many years ago.

To relate Tupac's story with the hero's journey, you can look at **THE ORDINARY WORLD** of Tupac Shakur as his origins and upbringing. Look at how parts of his mother's story on how she was incarcerated while pregnant with Tupac or how prestigious his family was within the ranks of black panther party and what ultimately transpired between his family members and the downfall of the black panther party as the hands of the U.S. governments' COINTELPRO program. Tupac's **CALL TO ADVENTURE** could be his interest in the arts such as poetry, theatre and music. **MEETING WITH THE MENTOR** could have been Tupac's own will and drive to carve his way into the music industry. His mentor being his own higher-self, guiding him on his journey.

Let's look at the death of Jimi Hendrix. There is no doubt that Jimi Hendrix is a global icon. His legacy proves that he is the god of rock music and throughout all his fame and success, he still died under mysterious and lame circumstances. There are tons of conspiracies about his death but the most compelling story of his death lies in the tools that were used to kill him. Official reports state that Jimi Hendrix died from asphyxiation but after further examination it was found that he was forcefully given huge quantities of red wine. The Greek god Dionysus' is commonly known as the "God of Wine." His main symbols are wine, ivy and grapevines. The color that represents Dionysus is amethyst. Before Prince came on the scene, Jimi Hendrix was already associated with purple (amethyst). One of his most popular songs is titled, "Purple Haze." Dionysus being the patron of wine as well as life, death, resurrection, intoxication, joy, magic, male energy, sexual healing and madness. These are all topics covered in Hendrix's music and life in many forms. Dionysus has a group of female devotees known as Maenads meanwhile you can just do a quick "Google" search and read some of the wild groupie stories surrounding the life of Jimi Hendrix. Even the way Jimi Hendrix died by drowning in large amounts of red wine continues to connect with Dionysus' myth; thus, connecting his divine power with that of a known deity. This should destroy any doubt and ill feelings about the role of your ancestors here on earth as well any suspicions about your divine heritage and origin.

Let's reel it back from the universally famous icons Tupac Shakur and Jimi Hendrix and look at the iconography that has been attached to my deceased brother Zandor. Based on the personality of my own brother Zandor I matched him with the Petro spirits within the Haitian Vodou pantheon. My family has a personal connection with the country of Haiti. Red is his favorite color and he participated in "thuggish" acts during his time on earth which is common for the Petro spirits. I found similarities between his name and voodoo deities associated with serpents. When he was younger it was often stated that he used to walk like a "dumpy old man" (with a hobble in his walk) which after further research, I aligned him with entities known as Don Petro and Prince Zandor; one is said to be identified with an old man missing a foot and walking with a cane. There's also an ancient Babylonian diety that corresponds with his energy as well by the name of Mushussu/Musussu. But overall, these symbols are what

I used/gathered to comprehend Zandor's power which finally led to acquiring his primal/soul name. You can look at other well-known ancestors and how they correspond with popular deities.

- Eartha Kitt – Bastet
- Bob Marley - Sekhmet/Nerfertum
- J Dilla & Nujabes – The Ashvins
- Ceila Cruz – Olokun
- And the list goes on!

The small list given above should act as a motivator to signify your own ancestors with the energies of any deity. Use your intuition when creating your ancestors' personal mythology. There is nothing you can do wrong. Your ancestors are near, always working with you. Also, don't get discouraged nor alarmed at the monotony of an ancestors' death whether they were famous or not. You and your ancestors are still divine and the power of such divinity can't be measured based on any definitions given by humanity.

Creating your personal mythology for your ancestors is simple, all you need to do is set clear intentions, be open, assert your willpower and have a sense of humor. Remove all doubt and any form of negativity because it has no place here – if you continue to remain fearful, skeptical and doubtful you are cutting off your link to the sacred realm of the ancestors. Remember that applying myths and fairy tales energize the souls of your ancestors elevating them to powerful spiritual frequencies, helping them grow, evolve and regaining their true spiritual powers – as more than gods and goddesses. Once their power is accessed, you're now a beneficiary of the same power. Empower yourself by empowering your ancestors.

IN CLOSING

"The underworld is open and the dead outnumber the living as the earth is drowned in waves of sulfur." – Unknown

Know that within you lies the collective power of all your ancestors. Deep within you lies the collective pain, sorrow and triumph of countless ancestors. This chaotic power is yours to utilize. Your dreams and your imagination are real! When contacting your ancestors and receiving information about their primal power, remember this: This is no illusion. Your imagination has the power to create any and everything you desire. You've been hard-wired to believe that your dreams and imagination are fake and ridiculous. But, you know that you've experienced the touch of your ancestors. All the information and messages you are gathering from the afterlife, the world of dreams, and the realm of imagination are "real". When you make the transition, you will once again live as your true primal self along with your ancestors.

The primal essence of your soul is expressed in dreams and the imagination. Your dreams are memories from the real world and what you see, feel and witness in this physical dimension is a dream. Know that you are greater than what you think you are, what you have been programmed to believe you are. You embody creation on all levels, your potential knows no bounds, it is endless.

OBSCURE ANCESTORS

The term and concept of ancestors is universal, carrying meaning across all cultures. Societies old and new have many titles and names they use to address their ancestors. Although the names may be different, the duties of the ancestors remain the same; to offer guidance and protection. Below is a list of various ancestors across many cultures that you can connect with that allows for further exploration into the realm of the ancestors. Please use the information below to add to your own ancestral deity system in any way you deem appropriate.

The Gedès

According to Judika Illes in her book titled <u>The Encyclopedia of Spirits</u>, she states that:

"The Gedès are a category of Haitian Vodou spirits. They are wild, rambunctious spirits, not easily categorized or pigeonholed. They negotiate between the realms of death and life. The Gedès are spirits and guardians of the dead. Some Gedès may be dead souls, but not all. They are sacred clowns from beyond the grave, spiritual caretakers of the cemetery. The Gedès are spirits of death and life. Masters of the libido, they preside over the start and conclusion of life. They have the freedom of those who have lost everything; they say and do anything they please. They are irreverent spirits who mock sanctimony and enjoy exposing the hypocritical and prim. They enjoy sex, ribaldry and obscenities. Gedès are rude, vulgar, painfully truthful and honest. Tricksters and social satirists, the Gedès are fierce protectors of children. They can be powerful healers, especially on behalf of children. Their specialty is terminal illness. There are countless Gedès, with more joining their numbers all the time. They tend to travel in packs. Some are famous, most are anonymous. Rank-and-file Gedès are often the forgotten dead, those without proper funerals or lacking descendants to honor them. The Gedès live at the crossroads and cemeteries. Symbols of the Gedès are skulls, shovels, grave digger tools, crosses and the phallus. Colors that represent them are black and purple. Key dates are November 2nd, All Souls Day. Favorite days are Monday, Friday and Saturday. Offerings they enjoy vary, rum infused with hot peppers, lots of hot peppers and extra hot sauce (to warm them up) and skeleton toys - the lewder the better."

The Bakulu

In Palo, The Bakulu are the ancestors. According to palo-mayombe.com;

"The Bakulu are ancestral spirits that transcended into the stars. These transcended souls are part of Kalunga, meaning, that which is complete within itself. When we speak of bakulu we speak of our connection to the world and the universe. When we call on the Bakulu (ancestors) in ceremony they partake of our offerings as living entities. They recognize our struggle and work with us to achieve balance and promote healing in ourselves, our families, our communities and the world."

In the book, Death and the Invisible Powers: The World of Kongo Belief by Simon Bockie he goes on to state that;

"The ancestors are the elders of the kanda (the proper term for a small section of a clan) in every imaginable way: chronologically, religiously, in intellect and in wisdom. Their name, bakulu, comes from the Kikongo verb kula, 'to grow up.' They are entitled to be respected, if not venerated. To become an ancestor means more than simply being a resident of Mpemba (the ancestors' world, a world without hunger, thirst, disease or feud) or guardian of the kanda."

The Great Old Ones

The Great Old Ones are a group of entities created by writer H.P. Lovecraft. It is speculated that these entities exist and are prophesied to rise and destroy the universe. There are many mythologies that correlate with this Necronomicon lore such as ancient Sumerian, Atlantean and Lemurian. A great occultist by the name of Brother Panic decodes the symbolism of the Great Old Ones in his book, The Origins of Occult Civilization Volume One: Hollywood. He quotes;

> "It is said that the Great Old Ones will walk the earth when the walls between the worlds begin to diminish and the gates swing wide. They are not of this world, but of higher worlds, they extend themselves downward into our space the way a man reaches into the depths of a pool."

Brother Panic continues:

> "We are the Great Old Ones. It is said that The Great Old Ones sleep in the dimension that is side-by-side with our own, which means the power, as described by the deities of the Necronomicon, dwells within us and it is what sleeps in the other dimensions. It is said when the Great Old Ones rise, they will destroy humanity. This just means when you come back into your true primal power, your humanity must die; humanity and your true power do not exist in the same reality. The Old Ones will then be able to claim their heritage as the stars complete their helical turnings and once more retake the throne in the heavens. The Great Old Ones are nothing but the melanated people of planet Earth, the oldest inhabitants of this planet and the parents of all realities. Another description of the Great Old Ones is that they are

124

godlike in power, but are still subject to certain laws of earthly nature. This is clearly talking about the ancient man and woman of this planet."

Nommo

The Dogon people celebrate an ancestral deity known as Nommo. Much of the information given about Nommo and other mythological deities should be interpreted symbolically. According to Robert Temple in his book, The Sirius Mystery, he states that;

"Nommo is the collective name for the great culture-hero and founder of civilization who came from the Sirius system to set up society on Earth. Nommo – or, to be more precise the Nommo – were amphibious creatures."

"The Nommo is 'the monitor for the universe, the "father" of mankind, guardian of its spiritual principles, dispense of rain and master of water. Not all Nommos came to Earth. The 'one' called Nommo Die, or 'Great Nommo', remained 'in heaven with Amma'. He manifests himself in the rainbow, which is called 'path of Nommo'. He is guardian of the spiritual principles of living creatures on Earth."

Temple continues,

"There are three other distinct kinds of Nommo, each personified as an individual. There is the Nommo Titiyayne, 'messenger (or deputy) of the Nommo Die, he (executes) the latter's great works. The Nommos who came to earth in the spaceship arc presumably of this class. A third class of Nommos are presented by O Nommo, 'Nommo of the pond'. 'He will be sacrificed for the purification and reorganization of the universe. He will rise in human form and descend on Earth, in an ark, with the ancestors of men, then he will take on his original form, will rule from the waters and will give birth to many descendants. The fourth Nommo is the naught disrupter named Ogo, or Nommo Anagonno. 'As he was about to be finished (being created) he rebelled against his creator and introduced disorder into the universe."

Faeries

Faeries have been around long before humanity. It may be that the word faerie may be a term used interchangeable with spirit. The Italian word Fata means Faerie; in Latin, Fata means Fate. In the book, Encyclopedia of Spirits, Judika Illes writes:

"Fairy is also the standard word used to translate amorphous, volatile, sexy nature spirits around the world, especially if they're female."

In Barbara G. Walker's book, The Women's Encyclopedia of Myths and Secrets, it states;

"Pagan gods and goddesses, tribal ancestors, and those who worshipped them all became 'fairies' in the traditions of France, Germany, and the British Isles. The Irish still say fairies live in the pagan *sidh* (burial mounds and barrow graves)."

Walker continues,

"Fairy mounds were entrances to the pagan paradise, which might be located underground, or under water, or under hills on distant islands across the western sea where the sun died."

The fate of all humans is death and the realm of death – the underworld is where spirits reside. The underworld is home to many worlds and dimensions, the fairy realm being part of countless realms makes it very possible for the title of faery to allude to spirit. To become a faery is to become a spirit and/or be full of spirit. The textbook definition of a faery is *"a small imaginary being of human form that has magical powers."* The imagination is what links you with these otherworldly realms.

Petro

In her book, <u>The Encyclopedia of Spirits</u>, Judika Illes mentions that:

"The Petro spirits are hot, volatile, powerful, angry and fast. Fast means they tend to deliver petitioner's requests quickly. Ask them for something and they will likely do it fast or not at all. (There are exceptions.) They expect that speed from others, too: the Petro are fierce, uncompromising spirits. If you make a promise to any of them, keep it. Quickly. The Petro are tense, alert spirits who crackle with energy. They are not calm or cool-headed. They are spirits who experience the world as a battleground and are ready to fight and win. Many love them because the Petro are vigilant protectors who anticipate the worst so [they're] always on guard. Some, although not all, will fulfill less ethical requests. The Petro pantheon is heavily influenced by Congolese traditions. Africa's Congo region was wracked by civil wars, tribal warfare and conflict stimulated by the early introduction of Christianity even before the slave trade. The Petro emerged during slavery and their ritual vocabulary evokes remembrance of this time. Tools like whips and gunpowder once associated with oppression are now wielded by the Petro. Fire- Petro are considered fiery even if they are water spirits; the colors red and black represent this pantheon - individual spirits may also have other colors."

Ancestors across various civilizations and countless centuries have gone by many other names with diverse descriptions and abilities. Use the information given above to forge a personal relationship with these ancestors. Remember that these terms to describe the ancestors mentioned above are just another way to explain your primal power.

EXERCISES
<u>Meditating on Your Guardian Angel</u>

This meditation is from Denny Sargent's book, <u>Your Guardian Angel and You</u>.

Constantly performing this meditation will help to build a strong connection between you and your HGA (holy guardian angel). Your HGA is one of your closest spiritual allies and they can be used as a mediator between your and other spirits. Before you begin contacting your ancestors, use your HGA as the beacon to filter out any negative or unwanted spirits or energies from trying to contact you. Your HGA will make sure you're communicating with the ancestor of your choice with no problems.

Relax and breathe deeply and rhythmically, sometimes counting in and out. Focus on your breathing and release your mind, letting thought processes and ego-babble simply run their course without attachment until your mind is quiet. You can sometimes achieve this through a single-minded focus on one specific thought, image, prayer, or sound to the exclusion of all others. When your mind is quiet, pray to the divine in whatever way you wish, in whatever tradition you are comfortable. Pray for the removal of obstacles, for self-knowledge, and for greater awareness.

Set a ring of pure white light [around] you, protecting you from all harm and filling you with pure, white light that banishes all stress and negativity. Sit and breathe quietly. Breathe this white light into your body and feel yourself filled with it until you are completely at peace.

Relax and meditate like this for a couple of minutes. Let the normal mental babble and millions of stray thoughts flow through your mind. Do not seek to stop them, but withdraw from them, let them go like eddies on a river, simply ignore them and hold yourself as still as possible. Let your mind go but hold to the center of your being. This sounds strange, but you will experience what I am talking about. Relax, relax. If you are in any way uncomfortable, stop what you are doing and try again at another time. You cannot hurt yourself or in any way endanger yourself if you are meditating surrounding by divine light! Relax!

When you are ready, breathe in deeply and silently say to yourself:

"Guardian Angel, come to me.

Then exhale slowly and say to yourself:

With Love and Will, so may it be!"

Pause, then repeat this breathing exercise for as long as you like – five minutes is wonderful – then let it fade away. Continue the slow breathing in and out and open your mind, heart and body to your Guardian Angel. It will come. No matter what you see or feel, stay relaxed and centered. Do not become emotional or try to force the experience. This is meditation; you are passive and are not doing anything, simply accepting the experience.

When the communication is over---and you will know it when it is—simply pray in any way you feel comfortable to the divine, thanking the divine for this gift and experience and asking for a constantly growing awareness of the divine and of your Guardian Angel! It is important that you let go of your desires and worldly thoughts during this meditation.

See yourself surrounded by white light and see it disperse or fade into Mother Earth. Slowly come back to the physical world and, before you forget, record your experiences in your journal!

**

To take your connection with your HGA to the next level, complete a ritual known as "The Bornless Ritual" which acts as a primer, jumpstarting your descent into the Qlippoth. A comprehensive form of this ritual can be found in the same book as the meditation listed above.

Decoding Dreams Tarot Spread

Grab your tarot deck and close your eyes, relax. Begin to focus on your breath. Once you're in a light meditative state, think about your dream. Remember as many details as possible. Remember the feeling of the dream. Begin to shuffle your tarot deck with the intention of understanding the message of your dream. Continue to shuffle your cards focusing on the question, "What is last night's dream trying to tell me?" When you feel satisfied, stop shuffling and split your deck into three smaller decks. Fan each deck out in a row, one by one until you see The Moon (XVIII) card.

Once you find The Moon card, remove the card that is before it and after it. The card before it represents YOU in the dream while the card after The Moon represents the overall message of the dream. Write down your impressions of both tarot cards in your dream journal. The more frequently you perform this reading, the better you'll become at remembering your dreams without the assistance of your tarot cards.

Easy Channeling Technique

Put on some music, any kind. It can be relaxing or upbeat. Pick music that matches your mood. After you choose your music, begin to mediate. Just listen to the music and zone out. If you need answers to a question, while listening to your music begin to ponder your question. If you're using this channeling exercise to communicate with ancestors, put on a song or music that reminds you of the ancestor you're contacting. Get a picture of the ancestor you want to contact and focus on it. While listening to the music and focusing on the picture, you will soon go into a meditative state. During in this meditative state, begin to talk as if the ancestor is with you and listening (because they are). Speak mentally or aloud, talking about whatever you wish with your ancestor.

Soon your ancestor will respond, their ancestor will come in the form of thoughts (different from your own, the tone will differ from your own), you may hear their voice near one of your ears, you may see images in your mind's eye or you may hear your answers in the song you've decided to play. The way in which your ancestors choose to communicate with you may differ each time you choose to contact them, coming in the various forms written above.

Robert Moss' Dream Re-entry Technique

This technique is from Moss' book, <u>The Dreamers Book of the Dead</u>. Use this technique to help use your dreams as a gateway to contact your ancestors.

1. Pick a dream that has some real energy for you. As long as it has juice, it doesn't matter whether it is a dream from last night or from twenty years ago. It can be a tiny fragment or a complex narrative. You can choose to work with a night dream, a vision, or a waking image. What's important is that the dream you choose to revisit has some charge –whether it is exciting, seductive, or challenging.

2. Begin to relax. Follow the flow of your breathing. If you are holding tension in any part of your body, tense and relax those muscle groups until you feel yourself becoming loose and comfy.

3. Focus on a specific scene from your dream. Let it become vivid on your mental screen. See if you can let all your senses become engaged, so you can touch it, smell it, hear it, taste it.

4. Clarify your intention. Come up with clear and simple answers to these two questions: (a) What do you want to know? (b) What do you intend to do, once you are back inside the dream?

5. Call in guidance and protection. If you have a connection with the animal spirits, you may wish to call for the help of your power animals. You may choose to invoke a sacred guardian by a familiar name, or you can simply ask for help in the name of Love and Light.

6. Give yourself fuel for the journey. Heartbeat shamanic drumming works.

7. Be ready to move into new territory. Your remembered dream gave you a doorway. It may lead to scenes and experiences far beyond what you remembered. Be prepared to travel into new territory, to have a conversation with the person or people you encounter, and to receive gifts of love and healing and resolution.

8. Record your conscious dream journey. You'll want to write about it and perhaps make a drawing or a map to hold the

memory of your experience. See if you can write a personal "one-liner" to express what you have learned.

9. Make an action plan to honor your journey. If you encountered a departed love one, you may be inspired to construct a personal ritual to honor them. You may wish to celebrate your experience in other ways. Dream require action!

Robert Johnson's Active Imagination Technique

This technique is from Robert A. Johnson's book, <u>Active Imagination: Using Dreams and Active Imagination for Personal Growth</u>.

The first step in Active Imagination is to invite the creatures of the unconscious to come up to the surface and make contact with us. We invite the inner persons to start the dialogue. How do we make this invitation? We begin by taking our minds off the external world around us and focusing on the imagination. We direct our inner eye to a place inside us, then we wait to see who will show up.

There are a few great examples of Active Imagination in literature. The Divina Commedia is one of them. Wandering in the dark forest, Dante falls through a hole in the ground and finds himself in the inner world. He is at the threshold of Hades. He meets the poet Virgil, who as he discovers, was sent to him by the beautiful Beatrice. Virgil guides him and talks with him as they hike through the various levels of hell.

This is a classic example of how to begin Active Imagination. Go to a place, describe it vividly and in detail to get yourself anchored there, and then see whom you encounter. In Dante's care, once he connected with Virgil and began walking, he met various people. You must record what spontaneously flows through you from your own special corner of the collective unconscious. For many people, this first step, the invitation, is a little difficult at first. They sit down at the typewriter, or with a pen in hand, and find that their minds have gone blank. If his happens, it may be that all you need is to have patience. Just wait, keep your mind focused on your imagination, and images will usually appear before long. To invite doesn't mean to manage. Everyone who begins this art has a lot of preconceived ideas about who ought to be there what these inner characters ought to say. People expect to hear immediately noble speeches by the Great

Mother or profound wisdom from an inner guru. These things often happen, but just as often we find ourselves looking at the depression we have refused to face, the sense of loneliness, emptiness, or inferiority we've always run from.

If this is what happens when you make your invitation, accept it. This negative material is the other side of your total reality. Now or later, you must dialogue with it. Jung said that it is exactly where you feel most frightened and most in pain that your greatest opportunity lies for personal growth.

BIBLIOGRAPHY

Bird, Stephanie Rose. *A Healing Grove: African Tree Remedies and Rituals for the Body and Spirit*. Chicago, IL: Lawrence Hill, 2009.

Bockie, Simon. *Death and The Invisible Powers: The World of Kongo Belief*. Bloomington: Indiana University Press, 1993.

Brother Panic. *The Origins of Occult Civilization Volume One: Hollywood*, 2014.

Conway, D.J. *The Ancient & Shining Ones: World Myth, Magick & Religion*. St. Paul, Minn.: Llewellyn Publications, 1994.

Cooper, Phillip. *The Magickian: A Study in Effective Magick*. York Beach, ME: S. Weiser, Inc., 1993.

Crosley, Reginald. *The Vodou Quantum Leap: Alternate Realities, Power and Mysticism*. St. Paul, Minn.: Llewellyn Publications, 2000.

Grant, Kenneth. *Nightside of Eden*. Bloomsbury, London.: Scoob Books, 1994.

Illes, Judika. *The Encyclopedia of Spirits: The ultimate guide to the magic of fairies, genies, demons, ghosts, gods and goddesses*. New York: HarperOne, 2009.

Johnson, Robert A. *Inner Work: Using dreams and active imagination for personal growth*. New York, NY.: Harper & Row, 2001.

King, Richard. *Melanin: A Key to Freedom*. Baltimore, MD.: Afrikan World Books, 2010.

Lemesurier, Peter. *The Gods Within: An interactive guide to archetypal therapy*. Winchester: John Hunt Publishing, 2007.

Levenda, Peter. *The Dark Lord: H.P. Lovecraft, Kenneth Grant, and the Typhonian Tradition in Magic*. Lake Worth, FL.: Ibis Press., 2013.

Lovecraft, H.P. *Necronomicon: The best weird tales of H.P. Lovecraft*. London: Gollancz, 2008.

McKenna, Terence. *Foods of the Gods: The Search for the Original Tree of Knowledge a radical history of plants, drugs and human evolution*. London: Bantam Press, 1993.

Moss, Robert. *The Dreamer's Book of the Dead: A Soul Traveler's Guide to Death, Dying, and the Other Side*. Rochester, VT: Destiny Books, 2005.

_____. *Conscious Dreaming: A Spiritual Path for everyday life*. New York: Three Rivers Press, 1996.

Ra Ifagbemi Babalawo. *Ancestors: Hidden Hands, Healing Spirits for your use and empowerment*. Brooklyn, N.Y.: Athelia Henrietta Press, 1999.

Ribi, Alfred. *Demons of the Inner World: Understanding our hidden complexes*. Boston: Shambhala, 1990.

Sargent, Denny. *Your Guardian Angel and You: Tune in to the Signs and Signals to Hear What Your Guardian Angel is Telling You*. York Beach, ME.: Red Wheel/Weiser, 2004.

Temple, Robert. *The Sirius Mystery: New Scientific Evidence of Alien Contact 5,000 years ago*. London.: Arrow, 1999.

Tyson, Donald. *Ritual Magic: What It Is & How to Do It*. St. Paul, Minn.: Llewellyn Publications, 1992.

Walker, Barbara G. *The Woman's Encyclopedia of Myths and Secrets*. Edison, N.J: Castle Books, 1996.

_____. *Man Made God: A Collection of Essays*. Seattle, WA.: Stellar House Publishing, 2010.

FURTHER READING

To learn more about the Dogon, here are some books worth checking out:

Griaule, Marcel. *The Pale Fox*. Chino Valley, Ariz.: Continuum Foundation, 1986.

Scranton, Laird. *Sacred Symbols of the Dogon: The Key to Advanced Science in the Ancient Egyptian Hieroglyphs*. Rochester, Vermont.: Inner Traditions, 2007.

_____. *The Science of the Dogon: Decoding the African Mystery Tradition*. Rochester, Vermont.: Inner Traditions, 2006.

_____. *The Cosmological Origins of Myths and Symbols: From the Dogon and Ancient Egypt to India, Tibet and China*. Rochester, Vermont.: Inner Traditions, 2010.

Temple, Robert. *The Sirius Mystery: New Scientific Evidence of Alien Contact 5,000 years ago*. London.: Arrow, 1999.

Learn more about the Qlippoth from these books:

Falorio, Linda. *The Shadow Tarot*.: Aeon Books Limited, 2004.

Fries, Jan. *Nightshades: A Tourist Guide to the Nightside*.: Mandrake of Oxford, 2012.

Grant, Kenneth. *Nightside of Eden*. London.: Scoob Books Publishing, 1994.

_____. *Beyond the Mauve Zone*. London.: Starfire Publishing, 1999.

_____. *Cults of the Shadow*. New York.: S. Weiser, 1976.

_____. *Against the Light*. London.: Starfire Publishing, 1997

Karlsson, Thomas. *Qabalah, Qliphoth and Goetic Magic*. Jacksonville, OR.: Ajna Bound, 2004.

Müller, W.H. *Polaria: The Gift of the White Stone*. Albuquerque, NM.: Brotherhood of Life Publishing, 1995.

Books on how to tap into your subconscious mind and interpret symbolism:

Farrell, Nick. *Magical Imagination: The Keys to Magic*. Cheltenham.: Skylight, 2013.

Henry, William. *The Language of The Birds: Our Angelic Connection*. Hendersonville, TN. Scala Dei Publishing. 2001.

About the Author

V.V. Gunn is a creatrix and wordsmith. She spends most of her time conducting occult research during the day and writing at night. She has studied English Literature throughout the years, graduating with a degree in Creative Writing. Her website, mysmajik.me is just a visible footprint of what goes on inside her mind; ranging from erratic rambling to info about new projects to bizarre spiritual breakthroughs. A naturally gifted psychic, she performs spiritual readings, uncrossing rituals and magickal workshops.

www.mysmajik.me

Thank You

To my brother Zandor; you continue to help me in this life and I await the day to be with you in the next.

To my spiritual teachers – Bobby Hemmitt and Brother Panic, I am eternally grateful for your guidance and all the work you've put in decoding and demystifying everything under the sun concerning occult knowledge.

All my love to my other-half, my best friend, my divine lover Brenston. You are my everything.

Thanks for reading! Please leave a review on my website detailing your thoughts and experiences.

If you're interested in attending a workshop designed to help those who want more in-depth information about the subject matter of this book; please feel free to attended my Ancestral Majik Workshop. You will get one-on-one training in Ancestral Majik as well as other information not included in this guide; along with personal rituals that I use to contact my own ancestors. I also perform reiki sessions/chakra readings to those who want more in-depth information about their spiritual energy centers including how to cleanse and maintain them. All of this can be found on my website:

www.mysmajik.me/

NOTES

NOTES

NOTES

NOTES

Made in the USA
Middletown, DE
22 August 2017